MW01067833

Teaching a Future President

Teaching a Future President

Equipping Students to Take On Almost Impossible Problems

Zachary Herrmann

ROWMAN & LITTLEFIELD
Lanham • Boulder • New York • London

Published by Rowman & Littlefield
An imprint of The Rowman & Littlefield Publishing Group, Inc.
4501 Forbes Boulevard, Suite 200, Lanham, Maryland 20706
www.rowman.com

6 Tinworth Street, London SE11 5AL, United Kingdom

Copyright © 2020 by Zachary Herrmann

All rights reserved. No part of this book may be reproduced in any form or by any electronic or mechanical means, including information storage and retrieval systems, without written permission from the publisher, except by a reviewer who may quote passages in a review.

British Library Cataloguing in Publication Information Available

Library of Congress Cataloging-in-Publication Data Available

ISBN 978-1-4758-4822-9 (cloth: alk. paper)
ISBN 978-1-4758-4823-6 (pbk.: alk. paper)
ISBN 978-1-4758-4824-3 (electronic)

♾™ The paper used in this publication meets the minimum requirements of American National Standard for Information Sciences—Permanence of Paper for Printed Library Materials, ANSI/NISO Z39.48–1992.

To my students, and to my teachers, and to all of the individuals who occupy both of those roles.

Contents

Preface   ix

Acknowledgments   xiii

Introduction   xv

SECTION ONE: A POWERFUL EDUCATION   **1**

1   Appreciation for Truth and Knowledge   3

2   Deep and Critical Thinking   7

3   Justice and Caring for All   13

4   Humility and Confidence   23

5   Leadership   29

6   Collaboration   33

7   Flexibility and Adaptability   41

8   Initiative and Creative Problem-Solving   45

9   Communication   49

10   Curiosity and Asking Good Questions   55

11   Resilience   61

SECTION TWO: TRANSFORMING THE CLASSROOM   **65**

12   Designing a Learning Environment   67

13   Classrooms as Organizations   71

SECTION THREE: MAKING THE CHANGE   **83**

14   Internal Conflicts   85

15   Either/Or Mentality   89

16   Recognizing Barriers and Constraints   93

17   Charting Your Path   95

18   Finding Ways to Flourish   101

Conclusion   111

Compilation of Reflection Questions   113

References   119

About the Author   123

Preface

I have a beautifully framed letter from NASA hanging on my office wall. The letter is set on the wall closest to my desk; it's the easiest thing for me to look at every day.

The letter is a rejection of my application to become an astronaut. It's my second letter of its kind.

I decided to hang the letter on my wall because I tend to have a typical relationship with failure. As it is with many of us, the risk of failing can keep me from trying new and big things. I decided to frame and hang the letter on my office wall to provide a constant reminder to myself to not let the fear of failure keep me from pursuing challenging, even almost impossible, goals. Perhaps, one day, I'll have a third rejection letter from NASA. We'll see.

This book is all about the types of educational experiences that can help equip students with the knowledge, skills, and mind-sets to take on almost impossible problems. Empowering students with the capacity to take on almost impossible problems is a worthwhile aim, albeit a challenging one. Indeed, the prospect of equipping someone to take on almost impossible problems seems to be an almost impossible problem in and of itself.

Beyond many other things, it seems like people who are able to take on almost impossible problems have two things in common. The first is an unnatural belief in what's possible. This would seem to make logical sense. In order to take on an almost impossible problem, you need to see opportunity and possibility where others don't or can't. You're more inclined to focus on the *almost* part, not the *impossible* part.

The second characteristic is that these individuals tend to have a special relationship with failure. Taking on challenging and complex work inevitably goes hand in hand with experiencing failure on a regular basis. It's hard to imagine a truly impressive feat that isn't preceded by several truly impressive failures.

Unfortunately, the reality is that many of us, particularly adults, have a very low tolerance for the risk of failure. We simply avoid situations in which we think failure is a real possibility. Consequently, we tend to shy away from engaging with the problems that are the most sticky and stubborn because that is where the chance of failure is the highest, whether those problems exist within our personal relationships, within our jobs, within our communities, or within our societies.

A great problem-solving advantage is given to those who have developed a special relationship with failure. These individuals seem to be less burdened by potential blows to their egos, which opens up more opportunities for them to try difficult things. However, "less burdened" may fail to give full credit to these individuals. They may in fact be significantly burdened and fearful; they simply don't allow those sentiments to keep them from trying. For many of us with *typical* relationships with failure, the risk of not being successful can keep us from even taking the first step.

Helping students develop an unnatural belief in what's possible and a special relationship with failure will be necessary if we expect them to be prepared to take on almost impossible problems. This can happen with meticulous effort in how we create learning experiences for our students. However, developing these mind-sets within our students is not enough. Being willing to be rejected from NASA doesn't qualify you to be an astronaut. It's necessary, but it's certainly not sufficient. The complexity and challenge inherent in the problems facing us and our world will demand far more from our students.

This book explores the role educators must play in helping define and pursue an ambitious set of goals for our students. Having an ambitious vision for our students is part of what makes our work as educators purposeful and inspiring. But defining an ambitious vision is not enough. We must constantly interrogate the learning experiences that we design and facilitate for our students and determine whether they are powerful enough to help us make progress toward our goals.

Many of us can look at our own life and identify a powerful learning experience that helped shape our knowledge, understanding, values, skill set, or mind-set. For some of us, the learning experience may have been a serendipitous experience outside the confines of formal education. For others, the experience may have been the result of a carefully crafted and skillfully executed experience from an educator. Unfortunately, for many students, these sorts of intentional experiences seem to be the exception and not the rule.

As educators, when we look at the types of experiences we create for our students, many of us can already identify which ones are powerful and which are not. As a high-school math teacher, I know that plenty of the experiences I created for my students failed to live up to the same level of ambition that my espoused goals demanded. Teaching is incredibly difficult. However, I can also point to some examples where I managed to get much closer and began to close the gap between what school was and what it could be.

An illustrative example came during one of the most memorable projects from my teaching experience, which was called "The Inflatables Project." During this project, students were given a hundred-foot roll of plastic table-cloth; a few rolls of clear packing tape; a pair of scissors; and a week to design, create, and analyze a giant inflatable structure. Imagine the type of giant inflatable structures that might stand outside a car dealership; these are the types of structures students would design and construct. Students' creativity was on full display as they created pyramids, frustums, and prisms.

One year, a particularly ambitious group of students decided to create a sphere. Unlike most groups that chose to design structures that were created with flat surfaces, this group decided to pursue a solid that would require a far more complicated design. The group ultimately decided to use the design pattern of a truncated icosahedron (the pattern used for most soccer balls), which included twelve pentagons, twenty hexagons, sixty vertices (points where the corners of the shapes connected), and ninety edges. The group had to determine the appropriate size of the sphere, given their material supply, and then calculate the appropriate dimensions of the constituent shapes. These shapes had to be cut to precision with specific side lengths and vertex angles, organized in an appropriate pattern, and then taped together.

Beyond the complicated mathematics required to calculate the area and dimensions of each of the thirty-two shapes and determine how to translate those dimensions into actual plastic shape cutouts, the group also had to navigate the complex task of working together to execute their plan and complete their project by the end of the week.

While I was initially concerned that the group may have bitten off more than they could chew, I was pleasantly surprised by the group's apparent effectiveness and early progress. Even though it's difficult to fully assess progress early in the week, because inflating the creation is the final step (the creation won't inflate until it's all taped together), it appeared as though the group was doing an effective job in keeping their thirty-two shapes organized and properly situated.

With one day to go, their heap of taped plastic was ready to be inflated. As the fan pumped air into their construction, the structure slowly started to take shape. It didn't take long to realize that something was wrong. The inflatable expanded to an awkward looking shape that more closely resembled a wrinkled bean than a sphere. Clearly, something was wrong with the design or how the shapes fit together. Considering that there were sixty vertices and ninety edges to align, and that it was all but impossible to effectively visualize their progress while they taped together the two-dimensional flat pattern into a deflated three-dimensional solid, it wasn't entirely surprising that a mistake was made somewhere along the line.

Since presentations were scheduled for the following day, I figured that this was the end of their story. I remember thinking that at least they would have a good narrative to share and reflect on during their evaluation conversation with a faculty member the following day. After all, the evaluation conversation during the exhibition was not supposed to focus solely on the finished product. It was also meant to explore the group's process, the challenges they encountered, both mathematical and collaborative, and what they learned from the experience. Given that, setbacks and obstacles could provide powerful fodder for reflection.

However, the group did not see this as the end. They came in after school to troubleshoot and problem-solve. They untaped and retaped. They went back to their design. They tried inflating their inflatable a few more times. Finally, sometime in the late evening, the group plugged in the fan and inflated a truly stunning and gorgeous sphere.

I was incredibly impressed and proud of this group's ability to respond to the setback effectively, ultimately leading to one of the most ambitious inflatables I had ever seen.

While students must ultimately be the ones who set and pursue big goals and effectively respond to setbacks along the way, it's important to recognize the teacher's role in creating opportunities to make it happen. My students would not have had the chance to set a big audacities goal and then struggle through a setback and collectively develop their ability to respond had it not been for the complex and challenging task that I had put in front of them. Had they been given more routine or traditional work while sitting in rows in a classroom, our classroom would have never given them the opportunity to think big and bold and practice bouncing back from a real challenge.

Educators must consider the types of learning experiences that will lead students to develop an unnatural belief in what's possible and a special relationship with failure, particularly if we hope to help them take on almost impossible problems. But those two traits alone won't be enough. Educators must also consider the knowledge, skills, and mind-sets students will need to solve problems facing themselves, their communities, and their world.

Acknowledgments

The ideas captured in this book reflect the knowledge, insights, and wisdom of countless educators who have dedicated their energy to supporting powerful learning for all students. It has been my privilege to learn from, be pushed by, and to grow alongside fellow teachers, families, schools, organizations, institutions, and, of course, students. As that learning continues, so too will the ideas captured within this book continue to evolve.

I also want to thank my family of educators, from my grandparents, to my parents, to my sister and her family, to my partner. Thank you for the feedback on early drafts, for pushing my ideas, and for offering your valuable perspectives and critiques. Thank you, also, for inspiring me through the work you do to support students.

Introduction

Imagine the first day of a new school year. You feel refreshed. Your students are energized and your classroom is clean and organized. Familiar characters but unfamiliar faces enter your classroom for the first time.

Amid all of the excitement that comes with the beginning of a new year, you entirely miss the truly remarkable moment beginning to play out right in front of you. There, near the back of your classroom, is where she is sitting. She is the future president of the United States.

Future leader of the free world. Commander in chief. Power and responsibility unmatched. And still, at that moment, she has yet to successfully navigate her locker combination.

Now here comes the question.

Three, four, maybe even five or six decades down the road, will that student of yours, the one spending hours in your classroom under your leadership, be prepared for the demands of the presidency? If so, will it be in part thanks to, or in spite of, the educational experience you created?

And what about the rest of your students? Will they also be prepared for their futures? Will they be prepared in ways that would make you proud to let everyone know that they spent time in your classroom?

As educators, we believe that what we do matters. Clearly, we have an impact on our students. What will be your particular impact on this particular child?

ALMOST IMPOSSIBLE PROBLEMS

What would it look like to successfully teach a future president? What would success entail?

During the 2016 Democratic National Convention, an advisor to President Obama said, "Nothing comes to the desk of the President of the United States unless it's almost impossible, and he has to figure it out" (Barack Obama—Democratic National Convention 2016 Film, 2016).

This is a bold statement. The only problems that make it to the president's desk are the problems that are too complicated, complex, or consequential to be figured out by anyone other than the president.

This begs the question: What sort of education prepares someone to become president, if being president requires you to take on "almost impossible problems" on a daily basis?

What would this education look like?

Every day, the covers of our newspapers and news websites are full of old problems still waiting to be solved and new problems that now demand our attention. Beyond the problems that make their way to the news, there are myriad other problems and opportunities waiting to be addressed. These problems may be unique to us as individuals, our relationships or families, or may rest within our communities or organizations. Regardless of size and scope, the fact remains that the world is full of almost impossible problems.

It's common to say that our children will "inherit" these problems. This sentiment is typically used as a rallying cry to build a sense of urgency among adults. Since it doesn't seem right to pass along to the next generation the problems we ourselves created, it's our responsibility to mobilize and address these problems, particularly the most pernicious and pressing problems facing our society. This moral imperative is certainly compelling. There seems to be an inherent injustice in creating and passing along problems for which you take no effort to address. Indeed, we should all get to work. Many people are trying.

However, as educators, we might also consider a different framing of the situation. Our responsibility doesn't end with solving these problems for our young people; it must also extend to empowering our young people to be better problem solvers in their own right. That's because our young people won't just *inherit* these problems; they will *lead the efforts to confront* these problems, and our question becomes, Are we helping them develop the knowledge, skills, and mind-sets that will help them to be successful?

Before going further, it's important to make clear that the message of this book is not doom and gloom. In this book, the term "problem" is used to describe any gap between where we are and where we could be. Consequently, not all problems are inherently bad. While some of our students will work on mitigating climate change or eradicating gun violence, others may build a safer and more powerful space shuttle or enrich the world with music and art.

Regardless of whether it's resolving a dire humanitarian crisis, curing a debilitating disease, inventing the next generation of technologies, or finding ways to meaningfully connect people across the globe, the problems that our students will face are challenging and complex. As a result, it's unlikely that any single individual will figure things out on their own. Indeed, solving almost impossible problems is a team sport. Are we preparing our students to play little league or professional?

TAKING ON AMBITIOUS WORK

To state the obvious, taking on almost impossible problems is ambitious work. It requires us to set ambitious goals and have the skill and will to pursue them. Unfortunately, many of us see a gradual erosion of the boldness and bigness of the goals we have for ourselves and our communities. This isn't necessarily an entirely bad thing. As we get older, we gain a deeper appreciation of the obstacles that lay before us and we develop a clearer sense of our preferences and what really matters most to us.

However, some of what is to blame for this decline may be more pernicious than simply "growing up." Beyond the wisdom and knowledge that temper and refocus our goals, less noble influences may also be at play. We may begin to lose our imagination or sense of what is possible. We may grow comfortable or complacent with realities that we used to adamantly reject. We may lose our tolerance for failure and taking risks, even when the risk is associated with things we claim are important and meaningful to us.

Wouldn't it be a shame if school was partly to blame for these evolutions?

Is a child's experience in school more or less likely to broaden his or her imagination and sense of what is possible? Is a child's experience in school more or less likely to embolden a sense of purpose and an ability to take risks and tolerate failure, particularly when the cause is worthy?

These questions matter, and, as educators who design and lead learning experiences for others, we must own the fact that we have a significant impact on the adults our students become. Therefore, we must develop a clear sense of purpose behind our education efforts and hold ourselves responsible and accountable for the impact they have.

ADVICE ON HOW TO USE THIS BOOK

The remainder of this book is divided into three sections. The first section offers a vision for the type of education that can help students take on almost impossible problems. Drawing on the insights and ideas from many others who have made significant contributions to this discussion, this section outlines broader goals we should consider for our students and the types of learning experiences that may help our students reach them.

The second section of this book offers a distinct way to think about teaching and learning, school, and learning environments. Shifting or expanding how we see ourselves and our work can help us be more thoughtful and creative in our efforts to create powerful learning experiences.

The third section of this book acknowledges the very clear reality that so many of our classrooms fall short of this aspirational vision. In spite of our deepest wishes and our best intentions, we frequently fail to provide students with the types of rich and meaningful learning experiences that do justice to our most cherished goals. In this third section, we consider the challenges that educators face as they attempt to close the gap between their aspirations and their reality and explore several ways to make progress.

This book can be read from cover to cover or by starting with the sections or chapters that are most interesting and pressing to you. There are questions at the end of each chapter that are meant to help you reflect and consider how to put these ideas to practice. The questions from each chapter are also compiled at the back of the book. While this book does not attempt to provide you with all of the answers, it does attempt to focus you on some powerful and important ideas and questions. You are encouraged to consider reading this book alongside colleagues, other educators, parents and guardians, and even students, while using the reflection questions to engage in discussions about where you are and where you want to be.

This book is intended for any educator, parent and guardian, student, or invested member of society who believes that education has the power to help students realize their full potential—not just for the betterment of themselves, but also for the sake of a world in deep need of maximizing the full capacity of all its members to take on almost impossible problems.

Section One

A POWERFUL EDUCATION

The role that formal education can and should play for an individual, a community, a nation, or a society has long been a topic of discourse and debate. Is education primarily a service for the individual or for the society? Should education serve to establish and maintain a cohesive cultural fabric, or should education be a tool to rethink and reconstruct? Is education a universal human right, or is it a privilege? If education is a right, at what quantity and quality should it be guaranteed? How closely tied should our formal educational system be with our labor market? Is the purpose of a "high quality" education to secure a "high quality" job? Is the purpose of education self-fulfillment and self-actualization?

Throughout the history of education in the United States, and in many places around the world, these purposes are frequently framed in conflict with one another. Indeed, there are some elements or implications to these purposes that can be hard to reconcile.

However, we are at a critical time in the history of education, our country, and the world, that makes many of these purposes more aligned than divergent. That's because, now more than ever, the types of skills and mind-sets students need to grow as individuals and people—self-awareness, critical thinking, problem-solving, collaboration, and communication—are the same types of skills students need in order to be successful in an inclusive democratic society, as well as the types of skills valued in many jobs and potential career paths. In other words, an education that focuses on serving the individual can also achieve other powerful purposes.

It would be a mistake to assume that the message of this book is that the purpose of education is to simply prepare students for their future. Education is intrinsically valuable and worthwhile in and of itself. That's because education can help individuals uncover better versions of themselves in the very moment, without having an immediate or apparent application to their future.

We don't always have to wait to see whether they graduate, what college accepts them, and what their starting salary will be to deem whether an educational experience was worthwhile for a student. Only focusing on the future reduces the powerful and immediate impact a strong education can have on an individual in the present moment.

That being said, the future is also remarkably important. Without a vigilant commitment to prepare students for the realities of tomorrow, whether they be high school graduation; post-secondary work; or their membership in a field, trade, or community, we risk losing the powerful potential an education system has to build better versions of society.

Education has to be about the present. Education has to be about the future. Depending on the quality of learning experiences comprised within a formal education, those two assertions do not need to be in conflict.

Preparing students to think about, struggle through, and pursue solutions to almost impossible problems can provide a way to think about the type of education that provides both rich learning experiences intrinsically valuable and meaningful in the moment and experiences that develop the knowledge, skills, and mind-sets that will be invaluable to students' futures.

While not every one of our students will one day become president, imagine the potential impact if every one of our students were better equipped to take on almost impossible problems.

What if we treated each child's education as if they would one day take on the responsibilities, and face the intense demands, of the presidency? How would our approach to education look different than it does now? What impact would it have on our students?

Imagine the potential that almost-impossible problem-solvers could offer to every field—whether it be medicine, technology, public health, the arts, or business—and every context, whether it be personal; interpersonal; or within a community, a country, or the world.

Unfortunately, too many students in too many classrooms in too many schools fail to receive a powerful education. When that happens, they miss out on the profound impact a transformative education can have. But they aren't the only ones who miss out. A deep-seated belief in the inherent potential of all of our children, coupled with the will and ability to provide powerful learning experiences that help them realize their potential, is what is required if we are to live up to the promise of our communities, our countries, and our world. We are better off individually, and collectively, if we all get better at taking on almost impossible problems.

The remainder of this section details several skills and mind-sets that will be vital to those pursuing solutions to almost impossible problems and explores ways we can work to develop them within our young people.

Chapter 1

Appreciation for Truth
and Knowledge

FOR THE PRESIDENT

In a world where plenty of "evidence" can be gathered or created to support any number of arguments, and when information is abundant but analysis is too frequently left underdeveloped, a president must have the interest, ability, and discipline to parse truth from fiction, fact from opinion, and thoughtful conjecture from careless speculation.

Nearly every decision a president makes is underpinned by some fundamental understanding of the world and how it works. Health and environmental policies are grounded in scientific claims. Economic and foreign policies are based on specific understandings of the current state of the world, as well as understandings of human behavior and what influences individual and group decision-making.

Your preferred approach to addressing challenges such as violent crime, homelessness, unintended pregnancies, unemployment, a struggling economy, and infectious diseases will be influenced by your belief about what is good and what is true. While thoughtful individuals can have legitimate debates about what is good, effective decisions are nearly impossible to make without the ability to analyze what is true.

IN THE CLASSROOM

Formal education is a particularly powerful venue to explore the concept of truth, in part because of the multidisciplinary nature of school. Students deepen their understanding of truth when they have opportunities to explore how different disciplines and fields produce knowledge and make arguments.

When students understand how different disciplines and fields construct knowledge, they are more empowered to be critical consumers of the arguments they hear. When students know the rules and norms as to how knowledge is created and how stories can be told in ways that mislead or narrow the scope of reality, they can construct their own arguments with greater skill, intention, and responsibility.

Unfortunately, we often fail to engage students in this way. Rather than engaging students in scientific, historical, or mathematical thinking, we tend to reduce these fields to the facts, figures, and procedures that were developed by others. When we do this, we fail to equip students with the skills needed to construct, and interrogate, knowledge themselves.

This distinction in how we approach teaching and learning is frequently referred to as the difference between "teaching students *about* science" and "engaging students in *doing* science." While teaching students *about* science may equip them with important and interesting scientific knowledge, it likely won't prepare them to observe phenomenon, develop and test hypotheses, and create scientific claims of their own. The same can be said about the other fields and disciplines as well, whether it be mathematics, history, or the social sciences.

Biases and Narrow Conceptions of Truth

Beyond scrutinizing the data we see and the arguments we hear, it's important to notice what data might be missing and whose perspective isn't at the table. Those who strive for deeper understanding must always ask how additional perspectives can help shape a more complete picture of reality. As author Chinua Achebe (1994) explains, "There is that great proverb—that until the lions have their own historians, the history of the hunt will always glorify the hunter."

When we only have access to (or only expose ourselves to) a narrow sliver of data and a limited range of perspectives, we can develop warped views of the world. Chimamanda Ngozi Adichie, in her 2009 TED talk, warns of the danger of a "single story."

When a certain narrative is repeatedly told about a group of people or a particular place, especially when it is told in the context of a power differential, the story can become our entire perception of that group of people or that place. As Chimamanda Ngozi Adichie (2009) describes, "I've always felt that it is impossible to engage properly with a place or a person without engaging with all of the stories of that place and that person. The consequence of the single story is this: It robs people of dignity. It makes our recognition of our equal humanity difficult. It emphasizes how we are different rather than how we are similar."

Even with a range of perspectives present, we tend to favor some more than others. Whether it be our own personal biases regarding who is trustworthy and whose voice deserves to be taken seriously, or whether we simply tend to be compelled by those who share similar experiences and similar demographic markers as ourselves, a true appreciation for knowledge and truth requires us to interrogate more than the data and evidence we see; it requires us to interrogate ourselves.

While we don't always expect future presidents to be active scientists, historians, or mathematicians, anyone hoping to take on almost impossible problems will certainly need more than a surface level understanding of knowledge and how it is constructed.

To do this, teachers can design learning experiences that actively engage students in the practices of their discipline. Teachers can ask themselves, "What sort of problems does my discipline consider? How do professionals in my discipline seek answers or solutions to those problems? Whose ideas and perspectives are at the table, and whose are missing?" For example, what does doing mathematics, history, economics, or psychology actually entail? What approaches and tools do members of these fields use to explore questions, and how are claims constructed, shared, interrogated, critiqued, and refined? Engaging students in more authentic disciplinary work will help them gain a deeper appreciation for knowledge and truth.

Upon hearing claims, even from an authority like the president of the United States, students can ask: What understanding of truth and critical thinking is embedded in this argument? In which discipline would this argument be considered strong? What data and whose perspective are missing? Am I convinced, or do I need to learn more?

Consider:

1. How do you help students understand how knowledge is produced within your discipline? How do you engage students in exploring bias and power within your discipline, and whose perspectives and ideas are taken up and whose remain hidden?
2. What opportunities do students have to question claims they see or hear and practice using disciplinary norms to evaluate the truthfulness of those claims?
3. What opportunities do students have to engage firsthand in constructing knowledge, using the approaches, tools, and norms of the disciplines?
4. How do you support students to surface and unpack the underpinning assumptions and beliefs inherent in the claims they, and others, make?

Chapter 2

Deep and Critical Thinking

FOR THE PRESIDENT

A president must have the ability to appreciate the intricacies of the problems facing our country and the world. Rather than adopting overly simplistic views, a president must be able and willing to see the complexity inherent in these challenges, see interdependencies between problems, and develop creative solutions.

The types of problems that reach the desk of the president are precisely the problems that others have struggled to solve. They are almost impossible.

The 2015 film *Eye in the Sky* details a multicountry military operation. When and how decisions are made emerges as a major theme of the film. The decisions are difficult for moral, logistical, technological, political, and legal reasons. At nearly every decision point throughout the film, clear arguments are made for competing positions based on different interpretations of the law, the evidence, the politics, and the conception of what is "right." Time and time again, when faced with these difficult and complex decisions, characters "refer up," passing along the decision, leaving it to someone with a higher level of authority to decide.

As decisions are "referred up," more layers of complexity are added to the problem. While someone close to the ground may have the luxury of focusing on one particular aspect of a decision (say, the logistics of whether a course of action will technically work), more senior-level leaders frequently cannot. These more senior-level leaders are stuck with multiple layers of considerations, such as law, politics, and broader geopolitical ramifications.

Consequently, presidents must be able to manage the complexity, the inherent dilemmas, and the interdependencies of the problems they face. In other words, we need our presidents to be deep and critical thinkers.

IN THE CLASSROOM

While not every student will face the types of challenges that take center stage in the movie described previously, it is fair to say that all of our students will face complex problems. Whether these problems exist within their personal lives, their careers, their communities, or their interactions with the broader society, students need to be able to navigate uncertain terrain with the support of their own deep and critical thinking.

As educators, how frequently do we provide students with opportunities to dive into truly complex problems, where simple solutions are evasive and new ways of thinking and doing must be developed?

To make this happen, educators must appreciate the significant relationship between the learning task and the student thinking that results. Critical thinking does not happen in a vacuum; it happens in response to something—a project, a problem, a dilemma, or even a question.

Students don't think critically because of an inspiring poster on a wall or because a teacher tells them to. Students think critically because educators design a learning task that requires critical thought. While this may seem utterly obvious to a philosophy teacher, tasks that genuinely require critical thinking can be all but completely absent in a traditional academic course.

What might such a task look like? Consider a short project from a high school math course. The learning objective for the unit is for students to be able to calculate conditional probabilities and expected values. A classic problem used for exploring these mathematical concepts requires students to calculate the probability that someone who tests positive for a disease actually has the disease, given the prevalence of the disease in the population and the accuracy of the test.

Given as a straightforward word problem, these types of questions can be answered in a minute or so and can become routine for students relatively quickly as they learn how to decompose the problem and solve it similarly to the previous ones. In fact, this is how math class frequently works for most students: students encounter a problem that they don't know how to solve, the teacher helps them through the first few examples, students learn the procedure, and then students replicate the routine.

To mix things up, a teacher might switch what information is given, and what the student is asked to determine. While this approach to teaching math is quite common, it certainly falls short in preparing students to take on truly complex problems that require their own deep and critical thought.

Consequently, consider how a teacher could flip the script and build off of this classic word problem to create a hypothetical situation. Imagine a fictional city that is suffering from an outbreak of a deadly disease. Two tests are available: a cheap test and a more expensive test. The cheap test is less accurate than the expensive test. Treatments for the disease are also available, and the treatment is more effective when it is used within the first week of an individual contracting the disease. Students work in groups to create a public health strategy for the community and determine who to test, how frequently, and when to administer a treatment.

To make the scenario more authentic and far more complex, groups are given an annual budget and the tests and treatments are all assigned a cost. Unfortunately, the budget is approximately half of what the ideal testing and treating regimen would cost. This means that students will have to try to determine the best possible testing and treatment regimen, given insufficient financial support. Students are given a week to work collaboratively in small groups to develop their strategy and present their plan and field questions from the class at the end of the week.

This was a real task in a real classroom, and students struggled mightily with it.

The math was challenging because of how many different possible conditional scenarios students could explore, and the conditional probability and expected values they would have to determine for each case they designed. (Incidentally, the task gave students *plenty* of opportunities to practice the skills of determining expected values and conditional probabilities, which were the math learning objectives for the unit.)

The task was complex because students had to work together to make significant and controversial decisions. Not all students within a given group might agree on what would constitute acceptable expected number of lives saved and lives lost. They were challenged to create and explore possible solutions that would push those numbers in the right direction and would have to decide how to allocate their limited funds.

Students also debated the assumptions and calculations built into their mathematical models and whether their results were accurate or not. Beyond technically mathematically accurate, students also faced the question of whether their solution, and their presentation, told the whole story, or whether it was at all misleading. The task raised questions such as, What information do we share? What information do we withhold? How do we frame our solution?

It's critical to note that the challenges these students faced are the very same challenges adults struggle through when confronting almost impossible problems in the real world. In that way, these students were gaining firsthand experience in what it felt like to work with others to take on difficult and complex work.

Student groups presented their strategies to the class at the end of the week. After each presentation, groups responded to questions and critique from their classmates. Rather than the feeling of a typical math classroom, the class was more akin to a congressional hearing or a meeting at the Centers for Disease Control. Students made legitimate challenges to each other's calculations, strategies, and assumptions.

This sort of project has the potential to completely reposition the role of the teacher. Rather than the arbiter of knowledge and truth, the teacher is now a fellow explorer, needing to pay close attention to the mathematical arguments students are making; trying to follow their logic; and determining the legitimacy, accuracy, and quality of their approach, alongside the rest of the class. Because of the nature of the problem, solutions aren't "right" or "wrong," but they can certainly be "better" or "worse," along several different dimensions.

Throughout the student presentations, the "best" answer was evasive and depended on the goals each student group had chosen to pursue. Students had to justify their mathematical and ethical assumptions and approaches, which offered another point of critique and criticism from the class. Again, these are the very same discussions and debates adults engage in when they offer ideas and approaches to address similarly complex problems in the real world.

One student's parent was thankful that her son had the opportunity to engage in such an interesting and complex problem. She said that never before had her son talked about math at the dinner table, and she was thankful that her son was engaged in school and learning in a way that made him do so.

Not all of the students responded positively. A few individuals commented on how they did not enjoy the responsibility of having to make some of these complicated decisions. Moments like these give teachers opportunities to help students see the value of what they are learning: if you aren't at the table helping make these decisions in the real world, someone else will be. Whether or not they are the right people equipped with the right skills and mind-sets to address these problems should be a concern for all of us.

Taking on almost impossible problems requires deep and critical thinking. If we don't give students opportunities to experience problems that push their thinking at school, we are forfeiting an incredible opportunity to build our students' capacity to work together to solve big problems.

Consider:

1. To what extent do students' learning tasks require deep and critical thinking?
2. How frequently are students' learning tasks routine? Can the tasks be completed by applying a well-known procedure or looking up the answer?

3. How frequently are students' learning tasks open-ended? Rather than a single correct answer, does the task require students to identify and work through assumptions, considerations, and constraints?
4. How frequently are students' learning tasks complex? Does the task require students to grapple with interdependencies, dilemmas, or apparent contradictions?

Chapter 3

Justice and Caring for All

FOR THE PRESIDENT

A president must manage the complicated reality of leading a country founded on aspirational language of freedom and inalienable rights, while also built on systems of exclusion and oppression.

In an ongoing pursuit to create a more just and inclusive world, a president must have a keen ability to understand systems of power, privilege, and oppression. A president must understand how rules and norms can be built and maintained in ways that create equal access to opportunity and success or systematically favor and privilege some over others.

A president must work to dismantle rules and norms that threaten the inherent value of all human beings and the right to life, liberty, and the pursuit of happiness. Given the many complex, entrenched, harmful, and unjust norms and structures in our society, this work will require moral fortitude and steadfast courage.

IN THE CLASSROOM

How can we expect our students to believe in the power of a more inclusive and just society if they don't experience inclusion and justice within their classrooms and schools? How are we preparing future presidents to serve in the name of justice for all if they are subject to inequitable and unjust practices in their daily lives as students? As educators, how do we build our classrooms, schools, and systems to model and reflect *better* versions of society and not replicate and reinforce the worst elements of our current version?

These are questions that many educators grapple with, some more explicitly than others.

While educators may have opinions and strong beliefs about what ought to be, many struggle to determine how those beliefs should translate to their daily practice as educators. Many of us may feel helpless in the face of larger forces outside of our control, and hope others can and will make necessary changes to address societal problems. While others certainly have responsibility and work to do, so too do we.

Understanding the Broader Context

Without our permission and our intent, society's ills can reproduce themselves in our schools and in our classrooms. Racism, sexism, homophobia, classism, ableism, and others easily permeate the walls of our classrooms, affecting our students and the experiences they have. While many teachers feel uncomfortable and ill-prepared to take what they may consider to be a political stand or direct action, inaction only favors those who already benefit from the inequitable power structures of society and harms those who don't share the same privileges. In doing so, schools help maintain an unjust *status quo*.

Educators must develop a clear sense of their values when it comes to justice in their classrooms and schools or they risk being complicit in the harmful impact of larger forces that affect our students and our society. Getting clear will likely require many of us to get more specific and granular on our values and purpose and what implications they have for the way we organize and run our classrooms and schools. It will also require us to reflect on our personal beliefs, assumptions, and ideas, particularly around issues of race, class, and other markers of difference. As Pedro Noguera, a professor at University of California, Los Angeles, writes:

> The stereotypical images we hold toward groups are powerful in influencing what people see and expect of students. Unless educators consciously try to undermine and work against these kinds of stereotypes, they often act on them unconsciously. Our assumptions related to race are so deeply entrenched that it is virtually impossible for us not to hold them unless we take conscious and deliberate action. (Noguera 2008)

While there are many perspectives on what the purpose of education in the United States ought to be, a widely held purpose is to prepare students for successful engagement in a democracy. Membership in a democracy requires us to understand our system of rights and responsibilities, as well as to appreciate the value that comes from difference and diversity.

Classroom Rights and Responsibilities

Citizens have rights in a democracy. Since those rights are not limitless, it's important for citizens to know the boundaries of those rights. Defining core principles, classroom values, or norms of conduct can play an important role in helping students understand how individuals can choose to organize the systems within which they exist. Rather than simply establishing a set of rules for students to follow, educators have an opportunity to build environments that actively support all students to grow and develop. Pedro Noguera (2018) writes, "Many schools focus primarily on rules and what kids can't do. They don't explicitly teach things like honesty, kindness, empathy, respect. Without those things, schools don't work very well."

When educators and students work jointly to establish and enforce agreements that recognize the rights of individuals and also consider the needs of the collective, students have the opportunity to experience the safety and benefits that can emerge from a space designed in pursuit of a greater sense of justice.

Educators can consider establishing a set of rights, responsibilities, and working agreements for their schools and classrooms. Rights can outline the entitlements that students have. These may be sophisticated, such as the right to be heard, or may be more technical, such as the right to eat food while in class.

Responsibilities can detail what students are held accountable to. These may be personal responsibilities, such as completing assignments on time, but they may also be responsibilities that contribute to the classroom community as a whole, such as the responsibility to help each other, to clean up after yourself, or to maintain the organization of the classroom.

Working agreements detail the specific ways the members of the classroom agree to work together. As Noguera (2018) explains, "It's not good enough just to have rules—you have to have norms on how we'll cooperate, how we'll listen to each other, how we're going to respond to mistakes." For example, a class may decide that it will always start on time, that every member of a group must speak once before any member can speak twice, and that all members address interpersonal conflict within twenty-four hours. Alternatively, the class may decide that it will always start class with an opening welcome circle, that students call directly on each other, and that interpersonal conflict is addressed as a full class. What the working agreements should be, specifically, depends on the particular preferences, goals, and circumstances of the school and the classroom.

Clearly, the specific rights, responsibilities, and working agreements held by a classroom can have a significant impact on how students experience the space and how classroom culture takes form. With deliberate reflection, students can come to better understand the relationship between how a system of rules and rights is designed, and the experiences, benefits, and shortcomings it affords its members.

While establishing clear expectations can be beneficial to all students, it can be particularly important for students who may have had adverse experiences or are experiencing trauma. Classrooms that are explicit about the type of respect that is expected, have clear expectations as to how to express frustration and anger, and establish the expectation for members of the classroom community to display supportive behaviors for each other, are laying the foundation to build a safe and supportive learning environment for all students (Pickens and Tschopp 2017).

Students can play active roles in designing these frameworks, monitoring their usefulness and impact, and revising them when necessary. Ideally, students can apply a similar lens outside the classroom to better understand how communities and societies are designed and organized and the impact those designs have on its members, as well as the community and culture that emerge. Experiences in designing, living, monitoring, reflecting, and revising a set of rights, responsibilities, and working agreements can help students build the knowledge, skills, and mind-sets required to be more active and intentional designers and members of the spaces they occupy.

Appreciation for Diversity and Inclusion

A democracy also relies on diverse opinions and perspectives to engage in thoughtful dialogue to make wise individual and collective decisions. The underlying theory is that diverse perspectives can help us chart a smarter, more enlightened, pathway forward, resulting in a better society for all.

However, it can take a great deal of will and skill to transform diverse perspectives into a whole that is greater than the sum of its parts. There are plenty of examples, both contemporary and historical, where diverse perspectives only produce contempt, hate, or even violence. Furthermore, there are certain perspectives that may stand in the way of creating a just and inclusive environment. For example, perspectives that assume the inherent superiority or inferiority of a certain class of people aren't the types of perspectives that stand to benefit a diverse group.

Helping students realize the potential power of diversity and appreciate the challenge of fully benefiting from it is a challenge that many educators face. Too frequently, students experience difference as an obstacle or conflict, rather than as an asset. Teachers can inadvertently reinforce these notions when they fail to help students embrace multiple perspectives or draw on students' unique experiences and insights. Furthermore, when ideas are presented or discussed as one-dimensional or overly simplistic, students may fail to appreciate the value diversity can bring to a community. Instead, teachers must help students understand how different experiences, ideas, and perspectives can actually be an asset for a community, producing new insights and knowledge.

To do this, teachers can design learning experiences that help students experience how we can be better together. Learning tasks and problems that benefit from diverse perspectives and opinions and that grapple with authentic challenges can help students develop a sense of interdependence and reinforce the imperative that we find ways to work with, and care for, one another.

Learning experiences that engage students in real problems and questions facing their community, whether it be related to alleged discriminatory housing practices, the quality of the local water supply, or how public space is maintained and used, can all provide powerful opportunities for students to experience the challenge, and benefit, of working through a complex question together.

Consider a group of middle-school students who worked through a masterfully designed project that achieved these aims. The project centered on a question of whether a new factory should be built in the local community. The students explored issues such as the number of jobs the factory projected to create, the risk of pollution to the local water supply, and the fundamental question of who has the right to make decisions that impact others.

Beyond the significant content knowledge students developed over the course of the project, it was clear that they also gained critical skills in negotiation, collaboration, perspective-taking, and problem-solving. Each student brought their own unique perspectives, experiences, and values to the table. By airing these differences, students were able to build a more complete and comprehensive picture of the problem they were facing, which served as the foundation based on which they could develop a creative solution. In fact, our society's problem-solving potential would be far greater if the dialogues and debates among adults employed more of the impressive skills these young students were demonstrating and developing.

Diversity alone, however, isn't enough. The mere presence of diverse opinions, perspectives, and experiences doesn't guarantee that the group will benefit from them. For deep learning to occur, students must also feel safe to take risks, speak up, and fully listen to and hear one another.

Depending on the individual characteristics of particular students, as well as the culture and norms of the classroom and school, different students may feel different levels of safety when it comes to taking such risks. For example, simply "opening the floor" for students to speak, ask questions, or challenge one another's ideas doesn't guarantee that it will happen. In fact, teachers who are attempting to provide spaces for students to express their ideas and interact with one another can inadvertently create spaces that allow for harmful patterns of participation and interaction to be reinforced. That's because students will likely already have deep-seated perceptions and beliefs about one another, what it means to be smart, and what school is all about. These beliefs can influence who participates, how students engage, and the way students react and respond to one another. Some of these beliefs will need to be disrupted in order for risk-taking to take place. What an educator does to establish productive classroom culture and norms matters.

Amy Edmondson, a psychologist and professor at Harvard Business School, researches the concept of "psychological safety." As Edmondson (2002) describes, "In psychologically safe environments, people believe that if they make a mistake others will not penalize or think less of them for it. They also believe that others will not resent or penalize them for asking for help, information or feedback." Edmondson argues that psychologically safe environments foster individuals' confidence to take risks. Consequently, educators should consider the current level of psychological safety in their classrooms and schools, and determine ways to build and reinforce psychologically safe learning environments.

Gloria Ladson-Billings, professor of urban education at the University of Wisconsin-Madison, identified and studied a set of particularly successful teachers in her book *The Dream-Keepers: Successful Teachers of African American Children*. Ladson-Billings found patterns in how these teachers approached community- and culture-building within their classrooms. Ladson-Billings (2009, x) writes, "They worked to create a community of learners instead of idiosyncratic connections with students they favored. This community building was almost always a result of deliberate pedagogical strategies the teachers used."

Respect for Others

Educators must intentionally design and lead their classrooms in ways that build a culture of inherent respect for other people. To make our communities work, we must embrace a constant commitment to learn and grow from one another. Doing so will likely require teachers to disrupt harmful and unjust patterns of societal beliefs and behaviors that are intentionally or unintentionally maintained and reinforced within our classrooms. Status hierarchies, harmful stereotypes and biases, prejudices, and norms and ways of working that systemically privilege or harm some students over others can't be ignored.

While stubborn and difficult to address, these dynamics must be confronted through thoughtful intervention and intentional design. It's not enough to denounce these things and hope for more enlightened and thoughtful individuals. As educators, it's uniquely in our power to design and facilitate intentional experiences that help students learn and grow to see the inherent value in others.

Consider some of the challenges that often emerge when students work together, such as predictable patterns of participation in collaborative group work. Some students will participate more, others less. Some students' ideas will be listened to, others' ideas will not. Some students' experiences will be valued, others' experiences won't. Some students will feel respected; others will feel dismissed. Some students will assume the authority to make decisions and manage the group, others will be expected to follow.

As many educators know, these patterns often fall along lines of demographic differences. Whether the patterns reflect differences in race, sex, gender, native language, perceived ability, a combination of these factors, or something else altogether, these patterns pose a challenge that must be addressed if a classroom is to provide a rich and meaningful learning experience for all students.

These dynamics have implications for students well beyond the classroom. Students' experiences in schools teach them about the nature of power, status, and how people work and behave in relation to one another. Elizabeth Cohen (1994, 37), in her book *Designing Groupwork: Strategies for the Heterogeneous Classroom*, argues, "If status characteristics are allowed to operate unchecked, the interaction of the children will only reinforce the prejudices they entered school with."

Through their work in school, students develop their own understandings of how the world works and how to interact within it. Cohen (1994, 37) offers as a cautionary example, "If the leadership position in groups always falls to boys, it will reinforce the cultural belief that 'girls can't be leaders.'" These problematic beliefs may have tremendous staying power and could stick with students once they leave your particular class or school. Skillful and mindful educators notice these patterns and work intentionally to disrupt them, attempting to create more productive patterns aligned to their goals.

In the case of harmful patterns of student participation, teachers may help students reflect on their own participation and the participation of other members of their group; empower student groups with protocols, facilitation tips, or sentence starters; provide direct feedback on how groups work together; and design tasks that ensure interdependence and collective accountability. Teachers may also have explicit conversations about group process and norms, considering those concepts as central learning goals in their own right, right alongside their content-learning goals.

While some teacher interventions may come in the form of introducing students to new practices, language, or skills, engaging students on a regular basis in these technical routines can also impact their evolving mind-sets, values, and beliefs.

Consider the subtle, yet thoughtful, change made at Mount Vernon Presbyterian School in Atlanta, Georgia. Tyler Thigpen, former head of the upper school, recounts a simple change to how teachers reviewed and graded student work. They simply added one line at the bottom of their assessment rubric with a question posed to the student: How did your work help someone else?

According to Thigpen, the results of this small intervention were significant. Students and teachers started making stronger connections to the ideas and problems within their classrooms and the ideas and problems outside in the world. Children became more empathetic, well rounded, and developed their collaboration and active listening skills. According to Thigpen:

> While we are certainly interested in the betterment of individual students, it's their collective successes and capabilities in the realms of empathy, self-sufficiency, and collaboration that are going to tackle some of the most pressing global issues sooner and more intentionally. We cannot rely on fate or luck to drive young people toward the levels of complex thinking required to create a more egalitarian and peaceful society. We have to embed that culture in their learning as early as possible. (Thigpen 2018)

Ideally, students in classrooms such as these will learn to appreciate the personal and social value that results from engaging in a community that constantly works toward a better version of itself—a community with the capacity to take on complex and collaborative work. This is the kind of classroom that we might hope would help shape the skills and mind-sets of a future president.

Consider:

1. Given your goals, what are the ideal sets of rights, responsibilities, and working agreements for your classroom and/or school? What role should students play in defining, living, monitoring, reflecting on, and revising them?
2. What messages do classroom and school practices, norms, and expectations communicate as they relate to the value of diversity, inclusion, and the inherent value of people?
3. What intentional strategies and practices do you employ to develop and nurture a community of learners and a culture that is safe for risk-taking?
4. How does the classroom and/or school model a community capable of taking on complex and collaborative work?

5. How can you support students to draw on their classroom, school, and community experiences to explore the impact that structures and rules have on how people experience a community and work together within it?
6. What systems and structures do you employ to help establish a classroom and/or school norm of respect and care for one another?

Chapter 4

Humility and Confidence

FOR THE PRESIDENT

An effective president must have a special mix of humility and confidence. She must have the humility to know when her fate is tied to the fate of others. Without this humility, she may be subject to the dangerous notion that she alone can solve the world's problems. The limits of a single individual are real, and the complexities of our problems are vast. A president must know when her own ability to solve a problem is insufficient and she must seek support from others.

A president must also have incredible confidence. She must have the confidence to know that solutions exist, even to our most thorny and perplexing problems, and that she is capable of leading people to find a way forward. Without this confidence, the first step toward addressing some of our most pressing problems might never be taken.

This unique combination of humility and confidence is critical for a thoughtful and effective leader.

IN THE CLASSROOM

As educators, how do we create spaces for students to develop in both their humility and their confidence? How do we help students appreciate their strengths as well as recognize their greatest opportunities for growth?

Taking on the world's toughest problems requires a high level of confidence. To wake up in the morning and approach the world with the belief that you can make a real difference for a real problem requires a level of confidence that is generally reserved for the very young or the very naive. However, the world is full of examples of people who do just that.

While having confidence alone isn't sufficient to be successful at taking on difficult work, it seems to be important for at least getting the individual to the starting line. Most of us don't even attempt a task if we think that it is impossible, or if we think we can't do it.

However, a high level of confidence can easily slide into an all-too-familiar level of bravado, if not appropriately balanced with humility. Rarely, if ever, are great things done by individuals alone.

It takes a genuine sense of humility to accept, and embrace, the fact that our fates are inextricably tied together. Our achievements are rarely ours alone. As Adam Grant (2018), an organizational psychologist from the University of Pennsylvania, explains, "Humility is having the self-awareness to know what you're good at and what you're not good at. Studies show that when you have humility in a team, people are more likely to play to their strengths. Instead of going for the spotlight, they take on the roles where they can help the team win." To make real progress on a meaningful problem, most of us will have to acknowledge our own limitations and enlist the help of others.

Acknowledging your own limitations, however, does not need to be seen as a failure or a weakness. In fact, if more adults knew when and how to ask others for help, we might all be better off. As Grant (2018) argues, "In the best teams, humility isn't a weakness, it's a source of status and a sign of strength." We might make more significant and meaningful progress on the very problems that are most significant and meaningful to us if we become more willing to embrace humility.

When leaders are both humble and confident, a combination that may at first appear as a contradiction, they can actually be more effective than if they had only one of the two attributes. As researchers Bradley P. Owens, Angela S. Wallace, and David A. Waldman argue in their research published in the *Journal of Applied Psychology*:

> Although an examination of leaders who are narcissistic yet humble may seem oxymoronic and even paradoxical, researchers have suggested that seemingly contradictory personal attributes may exist simultaneously and may actually work together to produce positive outcomes. Results from survey data from followers and leaders working for a large health insurance organization showed that the interaction of leader narcissism and leader humility is associated with perceptions of leader effectiveness, follower job engagement, and subjective and objective follower job performance. Together, these results suggest that narcissistic leaders can have positive effects on followers when their narcissism is tempered by humility. (Owens, Wallace, and Waldman 2015, 1203)

Unfortunately, the experiences encountered by our young people can make them believe that humility is a weakness, that collaboration is unnecessary, and that other people's success comes at the cost of their own. In an environment where individual achievement reigns supreme, those who fail to be at the highest levels of narrowly defined accomplishment lose confidence and those who achieve because they happen to fit the mold can lose their humility.

However, even the highest achievers will one day be humbled by the challenges they face. This can be a tough wake-up call and can create very problematic experiences for students. Ideally, the first time a student struggles or experiences a setback shouldn't be their freshman year at college, or their first day of their new job. In fact, humility can play a significant role in helping us become lifelong learners. As Grant (2018) explains, "Humility stops us from resting on our laurels. It prevents us from getting complacent. It keeps us focused on learning." Building a healthy mind-set around confidence and humility can and should start early, and educators can play a critical role.

Just like many of the skills and mind-sets outlined in this book, educators do not develop humility and confidence directly. They are not like basketball skills that you can explicitly drill, such as dribbling and free-throw shooting. Rather, humility and confidence can be developed in response to carefully crafted learning experiences. Teachers can help students develop humility and confidence through the type of work and the features of the learning environments educators design.

Learning tasks that require true interdependence, where students rely on one another because they have to, can develop humility. Any learning task where the solution is better as a result of diverse perspectives, knowledge, or skills can achieve this aim. If a problem or a task can more easily be done by a single, "quick," individual, then it probably will be. However, if the task requires individuals to lean on the perspectives, knowledge, or skills of others, then we are more inclined to see the limitations of our own personal resources and the value of working with others.

It should be noted, if it's not already abundantly clear, that most of the almost impossible problems facing our world today could clearly benefit from diverse perspectives, knowledge, and skills. Why should the classroom be any different?

While tasks that require collaboration can build humility, tasks that are appropriately challenging can build confidence. Students don't gain confidence by taking on easy work. They gain confidence when they make progress on work that seemed difficult at first, perhaps even impossible. We gain confidence when we make headway on work that exists at the edge of our current abilities.

Imagine the school advisor that coaches her students to choose goals that seem "just out of reach." Rather than encouraging students to pick a goal they think they can achieve, she encourages them to identify something just a bit more difficult. Even if the students are not ultimately successful on the "just out of reach" goals, the progress they make in pursuit of those goals could very well extend beyond what they originally thought they could accomplish. In that sense, failure doesn't have to be associated with losing confidence at all. In fact, it can be the exact opposite. Making meaningful progress toward an ambitious goal, even when falling short, can instill more confidence than achieving a less ambitious goal ever could.

To make this possible, students may need to shift their mind-sets in how they experience and make sense of effort and difficulty. Rather than seeing the need to exert real effort, and the experience of true difficulty, as evidence that they are incapable or not smart, students can learn to see these things as natural and necessary aspects of learning and growing.

To help develop our students' confidence, what if we only engaged our students in "just out of reach" work? Could it really be that simple?

While challenge is a necessary component, it alone may not be enough to provide the right developmental opportunity for all of our students, all of the time. Giving students "just out of reach" work must be accompanied by the right level of support. The right level of support may look very different for different students, depending on their particular needs.

Additionally, supporting students to take on challenging work may require teachers to actively work against the negative impact harmful stereotypes or biases may have on students. In other words, asking students to challenge themselves may require more than a mere pep talk; it may require the teacher to actively intervene to disrupt factors that are getting in the way.

Some students who have experienced traumatic events may be more inclined to avoid engaging in stressful situations (Pickens and Tschopp 2017). Educators must build meaningful connections with students where they convey respect for student perspectives. Educators must listen to, and value, the ideas, experiences, and perspectives students bring to the table and avoid making assumptions about why a particular student may appear resistant or why a certain learning experience may be challenging or difficult. The National Child Traumatic Stress Network offers resources related to screening and assessment. Educators should consult with their school, district, and other professionals to determine a plan to best support all students, at both the school and system levels, as well as at the classroom level.

In addition to stressors that arise from adverse life experiences and trauma, there are other factors that may influence how a student responds to challenges, setbacks, and opportunities. Consider Claude Steele's work on stereotype threat. Steele and his colleagues explore the impact that negative stereotypes can have on individuals who belong to the group in which those stereotypes exist.

Whether a negative stereotype targets gender or race, members of the stereotyped group are more likely to underperform when the stereotype is made salient. As the American Psychological Association (2009) describes the phenomenon, "A growing body of studies undercuts conventional assumptions that genetics or cultural differences lead some students—such as African Americans or girls—to do poorly on standardized academic tests and other academic performances. Instead, it's become clear that negative stereotypes raise inhibiting doubts and high-pressure anxieties in a test-taker's mind, resulting in the phenomenon of 'stereotype threat.'" As Claude Steele (2010, 5) describes the threat, "It is present in any situation to which the stereotype is relevant. And this means that it follows members of the stereotyped group into these situations like a balloon over their heads. It can be very hard to shake."

Fortunately, researchers have also discovered very modest interventions that have the potential to eliminate this impact, such as telling subjects that the test is not an indicator of ability or intelligence, or that the test doesn't show performance differences across race or gender (American Psychological Association 2009). In his book *Whistling Vivaldi: How Stereotypes Affect Us and What We Can Do*, Steele offers a summary of threat-reducing research:

> Their cohering principle is straightforward: they foster a threat-mitigating narrative about one's susceptibility to being stereotyped in the schooling context. And though no single, one-size-fits-all strategy has evolved, the research offers an expanding set of strategies for doing this: establishing trust through demanding but supportive relationships, fostering hopeful narratives about belonging in the setting, arranging informal cross-group conversations to reveal that one's identity is not the sole cause of one's negative experiences in the setting, representing critical abilities as learnable, and using child-centered teaching techniques. (Steele 2010, 181)

Teachers must be mindful of the harmful stereotypes and biases that may have a negative impact on certain students, and be disciplined and intentional with how they intervene, communicate expectations, and support their students.

Consider:

1. To build humility, what kinds of meaningful learning experiences would require students to rely on each other in order to succeed?
2. To build confidence, what kinds of meaningful learning experiences would require students to practice working at the edge of their current abilities?
3. How do you help students recognize their strengths and their areas for improvement? How can you use self-assessments, goal-setting routines,

and teacher- and peer-coaching to support students as they develop a special mix of humility and confidence?
4. What factors may influence how some students develop humility and confidence? What stereotypes may be at play, and what can you do to actively intervene?

Chapter 5

Leadership

FOR THE PRESIDENT

Exercising leadership is about mobilizing individuals to face complex challenges and make progress toward ambitious goals. In that sense, the leadership demands on a president are profound. Often needing to negotiate the very definition and nature of the challenges facing the country and the goals worthy of pursuit, a president must help a country see, understand, and take on the right problems at the right times.

Presidents are frequently admired for their ability and willingness to identify problems, direct people's attention toward those problems, and facilitate what is often long and arduous work to confront those problems.

Whether it be Abraham Lincoln during the Civil War, Franklin D. Roosevelt during the Great Depression, or John F. Kennedy during the space race, some of the most popular examples of presidential leadership involve the president mobilizing the country to face, and address, a common problem.

IN THE CLASSROOM

When students are asked about their leadership experiences, most students are likely to recall formal roles they've occupied in clubs, sports, or volunteering opportunities. Whether they were the captain of a sports team, vice president of a club, or helped organize a group of students to conduct volunteer work at a local community-based organization, it's easiest for students (and adults) to associate leadership with formal and recognizable roles. In fact, when a student hasn't occupied one of these roles, it may be difficult for them to see themselves as someone with leadership experience or potential.

Furthermore, these roles are also generally associated with groups comprising coalitions of the willing. While these roles can be powerful experiences for students and provide useful contributions to their communities, focusing solely on these formal roles results in a rather narrow conception of leadership.

After all, leadership also requires individuals to mobilize those who are far less eager. Some of the most crucial times individuals are called to exercise leadership occur when they have little formal authority or power, and people have little interest in "being led." The difficult challenge of leadership is helping people face problems they've been avoiding or ignoring or would prefer that someone else solves for them. This sort of leadership isn't always greeted with open arms and doesn't always come with fancy titles.

We all live in communities that face problems and have unrealized potential. While our communities could benefit from our leadership, the work of leadership is difficult, and most of us feel ill-equipped to take it on. As a result, problems persist and opportunities go unrealized.

While adults can struggle to successfully organize ourselves around these problems, it's quite possible that many of our schools aren't doing many favors for our future generations either. In fact, most of us could likely name more examples of students exercising leadership in spite or in defiance of their school, rather than actively supported and assisted by it. But what if our schools took a more active approach in helping students develop their leadership capacity?

School as a Laboratory for Leadership Development

Our schools and classrooms have the potential to provide powerful opportunities for students to practice leadership. If leadership is about mobilizing others to face and solve problems, we need to help students problematize the world in which they live. Students can ask: Where in my community, or my school, or this classroom, are there problems worthy of our attention? Where is the missing potential? What role can I play?

In reality, many of us take the tough work of leadership out of students' hands and place it into our own. Adults are typically the ones who define the problems and decide on behalf of students how those problems will be addressed.

Teachers must find ways to share the responsibility for defining, facing, and solving problems with their students. For example, consider Antoinette, a teacher who has grown frustrated by the lack of student participation in her class. At this point in the year, the same three students are the only ones who bother to speak up. No one else even raises their hand.

Antoinette begins to see her situation as a problem with student engagement, initiative, and responsibility. Students simply need to pay attention and step up. Consequently, she decides to institute a new participation policy that awards grades based on how frequently students participate in class. While the introduction of daily points awarded for speaking up in class seems to have a brief positive impact on participation, it's not long until the same old pattern falls back into place.

Antoinette's situation may be a classic example of a teacher seeing a problem, defining it on her own terms, and attempting to solve it.

Now consider what it might look like if Antoinette shared the leadership responsibility with her students. Perhaps she starts class by sharing some of the patterns she has observed and asks students to write down their own observations. She asks students what patterns they see with participation. Are they noticing the same things she is?

To better understand the problem, Antoinette asks her students to write the responses to two prompts on two separate note cards: "I choose to participate when . . ." and "I choose not to participate when. . . ." Once students have a chance to reflect and write, she has them place their post-it notes on the board. She then invites the entire class to identify themes that may exist across the student responses.

The themes that emerge paint a very different picture than the one Antoinette originally saw. Rather than the problem being one of student engagement, initiative, and responsibility, the student responses reveal a completely different problem. Students say that they were more likely to participate when they are interested in the topic, when the question is interesting (not a question with a single correct answer), when they have some time to think before responding (Antoinette calls on students five seconds after she poses a question, something she has been working to change!), or when they have a chance to first talk in smaller groups.

It's important to note that this alternative understanding of the problem would lead to an entirely different set of solutions. It's also true that the solutions that could result from this discussion are more likely to be effective and sustainable, since they more closely address how students are experiencing the problem. It's also possible that Antoinette's original definition isn't entirely wrong. Perhaps students truly do need to take on some increased responsibility. The purpose behind this process is to allow everyone, Antoinette and her students, to see a more complete picture of what might be going on. This picture can form the foundation based on which solutions can be discussed and jointly pursued.

Antoinette now enlists her students to develop some solutions to the problem. The more complete picture of the problem reveals that the issue of student engagement can't be addressed by any single individual or through any single policy. Rather, authentic engagement requires everyone—both students and teachers—to play a role and take on their specific responsibilities.

So why don't we as educators engage our students in more problem-solving processes like the one described here? Why are we tempted to define and solve these problems on our own?

Part of the challenge may come from our own understanding of our role as educators and leaders. We may sometimes feel that taking problems on ourselves is actually a fundamental part of our responsibility.

However, this notion of leadership may be offtrack. Leadership experts Ronald Heifetz and Marty Linsky argue that those in authority can be misguided when they attempt to solve other people's problems. Rather, they argue that a leader's role is to help others face the problem. They refer to this leadership concept as "place the work where it belongs" (Heifetz and Linsky 2002, 127). They argue that while groups will frequently look to an authority to solve their problems, the work must actually be done by the members of the group, since the problem is with them. Therefore, exercising leadership is less about solving other people's problems and more about helping facilitate group problem-solving processes.

Many teachers translate this concept into their classroom with expert skill. Whether students are struggling to work well with each other, learn or understand important academic concepts, or take ownership over problems within their school or community, these teachers are able to coach and support students as they facilitate problem-solving processes with their classmates.

Consider:

1. To what extent do students have genuine opportunities to practice and develop their leadership?
2. What role do students play in identifying and defining problems facing their classroom, school, or community?
3. How do you help students embrace their responsibility and develop their skills at addressing these problems?

Chapter 6

Collaboration

FOR THE PRESIDENT

Many of the problems most worthy of our attention are those that cross boundaries of various kinds. Some problems cross the boundaries of fields and disciplines, such as a groundbreaking heart surgery that intersects medicine, biology, technology, and ethics. Other problems may cross more literal boundaries, such as a humanitarian crisis that expands across multiple countries and has political, economic, and military considerations. Other problems may cross different sectors, such as the suffering labor market in a particular geographical region, which could be inextricably tied to decisions made in the public, private, and nonprofit spheres. And for some of us, our most pressing problems may be interpersonal, such as a conflict with a close friend or a loved one.

Problems of these sorts can't be solved by a single individual. They require people to find ways to work together.

The pressing problems facing our communities, our countries, and our society tend to be these boundary-crossing problems. They aren't isolated to a single group or entity. No one can solve these problems on their own, not even a president. Consequently, a president must have the ability, and willingness, to collaborate.

Problem-solving in politics is often adversarial. Competing sides with opposing ideas debate the virtues of their own positions. This process frequently leads to one side winning and one side losing or to a stalemate. Negotiation experts sometimes call this "positional bargaining" (Fisher, Ury, and Patton 1991, 3). When engaged in positional bargaining, parties trade and barter different aspects of their proposed agreement. The assumption is that there is a fixed pie, and the question is how the pie will get cut and distributed. When this approach is used, both sides attempt to get more than they give.

While a positional bargaining approach to working with others can involve a great deal of coordination and cooperation, it can also be a far cry from what is required to solve truly complex problems. Truly complex problems often require genuine collaboration. Rather than using cooperation to trade resources or barter for positions, collaboration occurs when parties codevelop a solution that is better than either one could develop on their own. Rather than a fixed pie to be distributed between the parties, collaboration can lead to *new* pie being created. Negotiation experts refer to this sort of negotiation as an integrative approach to problem-solving (Program on Negotiation 2019).

Very few of the problems facing the president can be solved through mere coordination or cooperation. These problems require multiple parties to come together to develop solutions that are substantively better than what any party could create on their own. While collaboration is an extraordinarily powerful and important tool, most of us are fully underprepared to truly engage in effective collaborative processes. As Barbra Gray (1989, 54), expert in negotiation and collaboration, writes, "Despite powerful incentives to collaborate, our capacity to do so is underdeveloped."

IN THE CLASSROOM

Collaboration is a skill. Unfortunately, for too many children and adults, it is a sorely underdeveloped one. Schools and classrooms must create learning opportunities that require students to develop and practice their ability to work together effectively.

Our attempts to get students to collaborate often amount to simply telling students to collaborate. We hang inspirational teamwork posters up on our classroom walls, we arrange desks into groups of four, and we even say, "Work together!" However, in spite of these well-intentioned efforts, evidence of true collaboration remains elusive in most classrooms. In fact, Gloria Ladson-Billings (2009, 76), in her book *The Dream-Keepers: Successful Teachers of African American Children*, argues, "Students may have opportunities for group work, but what teachers deem cooperative behavior more accurately falls under the category of compliance or conformity."

Perhaps the problem is that we see collaboration as the ultimate goal, rather than collaboration as the means to a different goal. Collaboration is a practice and approach used to solve difficult and complex problems. What if we saw collaboration as the means and not the end? How could that framing of collaboration help us make decisions of when and how to build collaborative skills?

Determining When to Collaborate

Collaboration can be a powerful practice, but it isn't always necessary. Teachers frequently ask students to collaborate when collaboration isn't required. Under those circumstances, it's no surprise that genuine collaboration rarely occurs. Most people don't collaborate because they are told to collaborate. Most people collaborate because the challenge in front of them demands collaboration.

Collaboration is a particularly powerful tool to take on complex and multi-faceted problems, because it's those types of problems that most individuals can't solve on their own. When an individual does not have the resources, knowledge, perspective, or insight to take on a problem, collaboration can make an almost impossible problem a bit more possible.

The power of collaboration comes from the diversity of perspectives, experiences, knowledge, skills, and insights people bring to the table. Therefore, collaboration is best suited for developing creative solutions to complex problems that no single individual could possibly fully understand on his or her own. As Ladson-Billings (2009, 76) argues, "Culturally relevant teaching advocates the kind of cooperative behavior that leads students to believe they cannot be successful without getting help from others or without being helpful to others."

However, even for problems that appear to be strong candidates for collaboration, it may be a mistake to assume that students should exclusively work together. Indeed, there is an important and productive role for individual work, even for complex problems. Some research suggests that being "always on" and connected with others may not lead to the best result. Rather, intentionally combining individual work with collaborative work can produce better results (Bernstein, Shore, and Lazer 2018). A thoughtful and disciplined approach to using collaboration within the classroom might also be welcomed by those who can feel taxed by constant interaction with others.

Knowing when and for what purpose collaboration should be used is the first step. However, teachers must also understand how collaboration works and the challenges that frequently undermine collaborative attempts.

The Right Task for Collaboration

Unfortunately, too often we give students tasks that don't require these sophisticated collaborative skills. Consider the English Language Arts teacher who asks his students to collaborate to complete a worksheet about a short story they read in class. The worksheet asks students to recall key plot points in the story. The task only requires simple recall. There is nothing to debate or discuss. The group does not benefit from the insights or perspectives of its members. The only advantage of working in the group is to (hopefully) arrive at the one correct answer more quickly than you could alone. However, as the students who can answer quickly know, the group only serves to slow some students down. This is not a task that requires collaboration.

The value of collaboration and diverse perspectives can be greater when tasks require creativity and may be lower when tasks are routine. Too often we give students routine tasks and encourage them to collaborate. While this practice is likely to result in lackluster collaboration, there is an even greater threat. When we tell students to collaborate on a task that doesn't require collaboration, we are developing an inaccurate conception of the value and purpose of collaboration. Those inaccurate conceptions can have lasting impacts.

Many educators themselves have negative memories of collaboration from their time in school. Furthermore, regardless of field or profession, many adults fail to have powerful and positive experiences working in teams. With so many adults failing to fully realize the powerful potential of collaboration, it's not all that surprising that educators experience difficulty in trying to create powerful collaborative experiences for their students.

Many of these challenges may come from our experiences being asked to collaborate on a task that wasn't the right fit for collaboration. Rachel Lotan, former director of the Stanford Teacher Education Program, writes about the concept of "group-worthy tasks." These are tasks that are worthy of a group—not just an individual. According to Lotan (2003), group-worthy tasks require complex problem-solving, deal with intellectually important content, require both positive interdependence and group accountability, and have multiple entry points, among other features.

Instead of the English Language Arts teacher giving his students the worksheet as described previously, imagine if he created a task that was worthier of group work. Rather than having students recall details from the story, what if the task asked students to identify connections between the themes of the story and contemporary events at their school or in their community? What if the task asked students to predict the motives of the protagonist, using evidence from the text to defend their assertions, and then write a short story sequel? What if students were asked to rewrite the story from the perspective of a different character, using a distinct literary style that is appropriate, given what they know about the character?

Notice the difference between these revised tasks and the original, and consider the different types of interactions that the revised tasks are likely to produce when students start to work together. Because the revised tasks are more open-ended, there is more to discuss and debate. Rather than being right or wrong, students can explore multiple possibilities, bringing their own perspectives, ideas, and questions to the table. Rather than seeking the "right" answer, the task asks students to explore complex ideas.

Designing a task that is worthy of collaboration is the first step, but it is certainly not the last. It's possible to have a task worthy of collaboration, yet collaboration still fails to provide value to the group. This is because most of us, kids and adults alike, are not very good at collaboration.

The Challenge of Effective Collaboration

While collaboration can be used to develop thoughtful and creative solutions to complex and challenging problems, things don't always turn out that way. The story that "we are better together" is rosy, but it doesn't always match reality. Certainly, we've all been in groups that fail to realize the collaborative potential that is possible, given the knowledge and expertise of the group membership. We've likely been on teams that have underperformed. What makes this happen?

What a group does and how it behaves has a significant impact on its effectiveness. In groups that are dominated by one or two "strong" voices, where individual expertise is never identified or leveraged, and where there is no real discussion or debate, groups tend to fail to meet their potential.

More effective and creative solutions can be developed in groups that actively engage all participants and perspectives, stay open to discussing ideas and alternatives, and create processes for facilitation and decision-making.

Supporting Effective Collaboration

Effective collaboration requires skillful facilitation, broad participation across group members, and the ability to mine members for the value that comes from their differences. As was discussed in chapter 3, unproductive and harmful patterns of participation will frequently emerge when students (or adults) start working together. Therefore, educators must commit the necessary energy and focus to support students to learn how to work well together. While doing so may require an investment in precious classroom time, it can be well worth it. Elizabeth Cohen (1994, 40) argues, "Teachers, particularly in secondary schools, feel so much pressure to cover curriculum that they do not want to take time to prepare students for cooperation. This is not a wise decision: In the long run more time is lost through disorganized group behavior than would be spent on advance training."

Students (and educators) must have opportunities to learn, develop, and practice effective collaboration skills. As Rachel Lotan explains,

> For groupwork to be equitable and productive, students need to make sure that all group members understand the learning task, participate actively, and contribute equally to the success of their group. Students need to learn how to

request help and how to provide help to members of their group. They need to learn how to engage in meaningful conversations about subject-matter content, and how to resolve substantive or inter-personal conflicts. Teachers need to know how to set up, promote, and sustain such groupwork, how to hold groups and individuals accountable for being on task, and when and how to intervene when problems arise. (Lotan 2004, 167)

The Social and Emotional Side of Collaboration

As many adults know very well, collaboration can put our social and emotional skills to the test. At times, the content of our collaborative work is not our biggest challenge. Rather, our biggest challenge can be understanding and managing ourselves and our relationships with other team members. Consequently, collaboration can provide students with genuine opportunities to develop, test, and refine their social and emotional skills, which are associated with several positive outcomes.

The Collaborative for Academic, Social, and Emotional Learning (CASEL) offers a helpful framework to consider the elements that encompass social and emotional learning: self-awareness, self-management, social awareness, relationship skills, and responsible decision-making (CASEL 2017). Teachers who strive to develop effective collaborators pay close attention to how these skills are developing within their students and provide ongoing supports, resources, interventions, and opportunities for students to reflect on their progress.

Effective and safe collaboration between students can face additional hurdles, depending on the particular experiences of students. As Pedro Noguera (2018) explains, "Whenever we broaden the lens through which we view children to go beyond strict academics, to look at their social-emotional needs or physical needs, we're forced to grapple with issues of equity. That is, we know that some kids come to school with greater needs (as a result of trauma or anxiety, for example) and that addressing and responding to those needs is a key part of ensuring that they have an opportunity to learn."

Students who have experienced adverse life events or trauma may initially find it difficult to work with others and build close relationships (Pickens and Tschopp 2017). Without understanding the potential causes for the behavior, student resistance, a lack of focus, or interpersonal conflict can be interpreted by educators as merely disrespectful or immature behavior rather than behavior that stems from other, more complicated factors. Educators must be mindful to explore possible triggers that may lead to traumatic stress reactions, and work with students, families, and other professionals to create learning environments that enable all students to be successful.

Imagine what could be possible if students developed a healthy and productive disposition toward collaboration at an early age and that disposition persisted into adulthood. Imagine the impact of our collective problem-solving potential if people better understood how and when to collaborate with each other.

Consider:

1. To what extent do students' learning experiences require them to practice collaboration? Do students solely work together on tasks that don't require collaboration, or do they have opportunities to engage in group-worthy tasks?
2. How do you explicitly teach students to work more effectively with one another? When you observe students working together, what are you looking for, and what kinds of supports (and interventions) do you provide?
3. How do you support students' social-emotional learning, including self-awareness, self-management, social awareness, relationship skills, and responsible decision-making?

Chapter 7

Flexibility and Adaptability

FOR THE PRESIDENT

While taking on almost impossible problems, a president must have the ability to recognize changes in circumstances and changes in the environment, and adjust accordingly. Rarely do things go as planned, or problems and circumstances stay consistent, particularly when navigating through complex challenges and systems.

When trying to explore or confront a complex problem, new information can be discovered, additional constraints can surface, and initial strategies and ideas can be put to the test. Sometimes these new learnings may inform necessary changes to a strategy or the options that should be considered. Other times, new learnings may dictate entirely new understandings of the nature of the problem to be addressed.

While leaders often feel the pressure to be seen as consistent and predictable, true leadership around complex problems may require them to be flexible and adaptive. Uncertainty and unpredictability are part of the very nature of almost impossible problems. Therefore, a president must have the ability, will, and courage to be adaptive and flexible when it comes to facing challenges.

IN THE CLASSROOM

While predictability and consistency certainly have their place in school, a learning environment that is too strongly characterized by these traits can stifle growth by failing to provide students with opportunities to react and adapt to changes. Intentional and carefully designed uncertainty and volatility in classroom tasks and learning experiences can provide powerful opportunities for students to develop these skills.

We often admire people who are able to think quickly on their feet, gracefully react to setbacks, and stay afloat despite of what the world throws at them. While life gives many of us enough opportunities to practice these skills, rarely are learning experiences carefully designed to help students develop them.

Flexibility and adaptability are skills that are called upon based on challenges in an individual's environment. While many students experience a great deal of challenge in their daily lives outside of school, often those challenges are not thoughtfully and intentionally designed to be a supportive learning experience for students. Therefore, whether students develop productive responses to these stressors, or unproductive responses, is left up to individual circumstances rather than intentional design.

The same reality exists within schools as well. Students might experience a great deal of challenge in school, but the challenge is not the product of the thoughtful and intentional design of educators, and critical student supports aren't in place to help transform the challenge into a powerful learning opportunity for the student. On the other extreme, some students may rarely experience any genuine challenges in school and consequently aren't required to respond to anything at all. If the biggest challenge a student encounters is forgetting to bring a No. 2 pencil, they are unlikely to have many authentic opportunities to practice flexibility and adaptability.

To help students build their flexibility and adaptability, educators must consider the types of learning experiences that will require students to face, and work to overcome, authentic setbacks and challenges. Educators also must consider their students and the level of support they will need to successfully and safely respond to challenges and setbacks. After all, a predictable classroom environment can help build a safe learning space, particularly for those students who may have experienced trauma or other adverse life events (Pickens and Tschopp 2017).

As experienced teachers know, there will be no shortage of setbacks and challenges when students work on complex tasks in collaborative groups. Indeed, these challenges are cited as the reasons why many teachers steer clear of these sorts of learning experiences in the first place.

When collaborating or working with complex material, the learning environment can get very messy. Many students (and teachers!) struggle to effectively navigate that messiness. In relinquishing some control to their students, teachers frequently witness students who are ill-equipped to work effectively together. Whether students fail to stay engaged, communicate effectively, work collaboratively, or whether they simply struggle to dig into the rich questions of the learning task, teachers fear that these obstacles will be too big for their students to successfully navigate without their direct control. Sometimes, they may be right.

Instead of seeing this struggle as a reason to retreat, however, teachers can see this struggle as an opportunity to build students' skills in flexibility and adaptability. Encountering an unexpected problem or challenge shouldn't be a signal to lean back, but it should be a signal to lean in. If we expect this sort of perseverance from our students, we must also expect this of ourselves, as educators.

The messiness of collaborative work is welcomed by a teacher who has a goal of developing her students' flexibility and adaptability. That's because the messiness provides genuine opportunities for students to experience authentic challenges inherent in difficult work and explore ways to get better at navigating those obstacles.

A teacher's role in helping students build flexibility and adaptability can be to support students in crafting their own responses to the challenges they face. Teachers can pose questions that help a student think through the situation, develop a set of options for moving forward, and choose a course of action. Unfortunately, teachers can be too quick to step in and solve problems for their students, as we discussed in chapter 5. In an effort to be helpful, teachers take on the challenge that students could benefit from working through themselves. It does not take long for students to develop a dependence on their teacher to solve their problems.

Rather than taking on students' challenges, consider an alternative. What could it look like for a teacher to help students think through and solve their own problems? When students show up to class without an assignment, when they struggle to reach consensus within their group, when they encounter a significant setback on a project, or when they feel disengaged from class and school, instead of the teacher telling the student what they think the student should do, what if the teacher asked questions and probed the student to think through the problem? By putting the onus of working through the problem back in the students' hands, students are given an opportunity to practice being flexible and adaptable.

Of course, teachers have an important role to play. Putting the onus of working through the problem back on the student doesn't mean that the teacher is absent in the process. Instead, a teacher can help a student reflect on what happened, brainstorm ideas of how to address the challenge, and support the student in developing a set of actions. There is a big difference between a teacher providing coaching support that actually *builds the capacity of the student* and a teacher telling a student what to do. While there may be times when the latter is necessary, it's unlikely that students will have rich opportunities to develop and practice their flexibility and adaptability skills if that is the only approach they ever experience in school. When engaged in conversations such as these, teachers can consider questions such as, What will the impact of this conversation be on this student? Is this conversation building this students' capacity to think through and address future challenges or not?

If we want our students to build their flexibility and adaptability, teachers must create environments where students are encouraged to set bold goals, and where their success will likely require them to respond effectively to roadblocks and challenges they face along the way. This environment must also include the appropriate level of coaching and support.

Educators can help students reflect on and make sense of their obstacles, brainstorm possible options, and select ways to move forward. This can all be done through thoughtful coaching questions that respect the students as the ultimate owners of the problem and therefore the owners of the solution.

Consider:

1. Are students' learning experiences likely to produce opportunities for them to practice their flexibility and adaptability?
2. When students face a setback, how do you, as an educator, respond? Instead of solving the problem for them, how might you coach them to think through the problem and develop a solution for themselves?
3. How do you support individuals and groups as they encounter challenges, so the messiness of the challenge is used as an opportunity to learn, not a distraction from their learning?
4. What impact might classroom and school policies and practices (e.g., assessment and grading policies and practices, individual and group reflection practices) have on students' opportunities and willingness to practice flexibility and adaptability?

Chapter 8

Initiative and Creative Problem-Solving

FOR THE PRESIDENT

A president must know when to take action and seize an opportunity, even if it requires her to venture into uncharted territory. Most pressing problems don't solve themselves. Progress requires intentional action and creative problem-solving.

Seeing the opportunities within challenges and having the will and ability to pursue creative solutions is a critical skill for any world leader.

Similarly, students must be supported to take action on issues and concerns important to them and garner the collaborative support of others as they pursue creative solutions.

IN THE CLASSROOM

In school, teachers typically assign students work to complete. Whether be they problems in math, a novel in English, or an experiment in science, the work is predetermined by the time it lands on a student's desk. However, for leaders and problem solvers in the real world, much of the work itself entails asking questions and determining what the work actually is.

Leaders aren't given nicely packaged problems to solve. Rather, leaders must scan their environment; identify and define problems; analyze the causes, implications, and constraints; and make a decision to actively take on a problem or pursue an opportunity. Defining the problem is frequently touted as the most significant and challenging work.

The book *Creative Problem Solving and Opportunity Finding,* written by J. Daniel Couger, recounts a famous quote frequently attributed to Albert

Einstein. According to Couger (1995, 178), Einstein "was once asked: 'If you have one hour to save the world, how would you spend that hour?' He replied, 'I would spend 55 minutes defining the problem and then five minutes solving it.'"

Entrepreneurs know this well. Their success relies on defining problems in ways that others haven't. "What's the problem you're trying to solve?" is a classic question for creative problem solvers. Most people tend to jump to a solution before fully understanding the problem. In fact, this approach is sometimes referred to as "a solution in search of a problem." Effective problem-solving requires more time and attention within the problem-defining space. Some of the most creative and effective solutions come from alternative definitions to the problem.

Consider the illustrative example put forth by Thomas Wedell-Wedellsborg in his 2017 *Harvard Business Review* article, "Are You Solving the Right Problems?" Wedell-Wedellsborg describes a scenario centered on a slow elevator in an apartment building. With residents complaining about their wait time every morning to exit the building, the most obvious way to define the problem is that the elevator is too slow. This problem definition points to a rather singular solution—fix or update the elevator so the amount of time residents wait will be reduced.

Given this scenario, many of us would quickly jump to the solution space. Our attention and energy would focus on when and how we could get the elevator fixed. While there may be some room for creativity in how we fix a slow-moving elevator, all of our solutions will be based on the fundamental assumption that the elevator's speed is the root of the problem.

However, a thoughtful problem solver stays in the problem-defining space for a longer period of time. That's because thoughtful problem solvers have developed the discipline to generate multiple alternative definitions of the problem. Maybe the problem isn't the speed of the elevator but the impatience or boredom of the residents. Or maybe the problem is the dark and smelly stairwell that no one wants to use. Or maybe it's something else.

It's not always a question of which is the "real" problem—in fact, all of the previous problem definitions may describe a "real" problem—but rather which is the best problem to try to solve. Surely, if the problem is that the elevator is too old or slow, the obvious solution is to fix or update the elevator. However, what if the problem is defined as waiting for the elevator is too boring? In that case, simply installing mirrors, playing music, or installing hand sanitizer stations in the elevator lobbies could solve the problem (Wedell-Wedellsborg 2017).

Identifying, defining, and solving problems don't just take creativity and skill. Problem-solving also takes initiative. Not everyone acts like entrepreneurs; we aren't all scanning our world, looking for problems to solve in new and creative ways. Individuals must have some element of internal drive to see opportunities and take action on them. Our society admires individuals who create products, solutions, or services that help solve problems, particularly when they do it well.

Unfortunately, students get little to no opportunity to develop these skills in most schools. Rather than identifying problems themselves, students are given them. Rather than developing creative solutions, students are asked to replicate procedures or ideas that they were taught by someone else.

Some might say that our current educational practices are the types of things we would do if we were intentionally trying to *avoid* the development of initiative and creative problem-solving. So what's the alternative? What sort of learning experiences could educators design if they were intentionally trying to develop initiative and creative problem-solving?

Giving students opportunities to develop initiative does not necessarily require the design of a new course or an exorbitant investment of time or money. While some schools opt to develop new courses in entrepreneurship, build design labs or makerspaces, or create other opportunities that are "extracurricular," there is great potential to infuse meaningful opportunities to develop these skills and mind-sets within the more traditional curriculum.

In fact, we would do our students a disservice if they started to believe that initiative and creative problem-solving were reserved for particular spaces like design labs and makerspaces, and had no place in disciplines like history or mathematics.

Teachers can make modest changes to their current approach to teaching that can have profound results. For example, consider a history teacher who has students analyze primary source documents in order to define the major problems facing Abraham Lincoln during the Civil War and then has students work in small teams to draft a "memo to the president" to advise Lincoln on his options.

Consider the science teacher who solicits possible research questions about projectile motion from students and then has students design scientifically sound experiments to gather data and develop conjectures.

Consider the social studies teacher who has her students identify a community concern important to them, conduct research, develop solutions, and then write an op-ed for the local paper.

Each of these examples requires students to take a more active role in defining a problem and pursuing a solution, something that most students have few opportunities to do.

Consider:

1. What opportunities do students have to scan their environment, identify problems, and work to build creative solutions?
2. How do you help students develop the discipline to stay longer in the problem-defining space before jumping to solutions?
3. How do you encourage students to take initiative to pursue solutions to problems for which they have passion?

Chapter 9

Communication

FOR THE PRESIDENT

A president relies on adept communication skills to convey complex and important ideas to a variety of stakeholders across a variety of mediums. In some instances, the greatest power a president may have is the ability to use a platform to communicate a message.

Beyond communicating externally, a president relies on strong communication skills while working with his team. How a team communicates, asks questions, and makes decisions all play a role in the team's ability to work together effectively.

IN THE CLASSROOM

Students must be given frequent opportunities to share their ideas and develop their communication skills across purposes, disciplines, formats, and media.

Leaders are often heralded, or lambasted, for their ability to effectively communicate. While some may attribute communication skills to natural or born ability, educators know better. Educators can play a proactive and intentional role in building our students' communication skills.

Opportunities for Students to Communicate

Unfortunately, in far too many classrooms, communication happens one way: from the teacher to the students. Communication, like all skills, only gets better through cycles of practice, feedback, and reflection. While some students have opportunities to communicate in front of their teacher or peers, it's typically reserved for high-stakes situations such as a student delivering a speech or presenting to the class. Without regular opportunities for students to practice expressing their ideas to others, receiving feedback, and practicing again, it's hard to imagine that much improvement will happen.

Having students produce and deliver a speech provides a clear opportunity to give feedback to help students improve their communication, particularly when the content of the speech is complex, controversial, or requires persuasion. Many educators are masterful at providing clear and specific feedback, based on explicit criteria for effective communication. Many others also engage students in a peer feedback process, allowing the entire class community to further develop their understanding of what constitutes effective communication.

However, much of the challenge in effective communication happens when students are not delivering prepared remarks. Communication challenges abound when students are interacting with each other, often in pairs or small groups, to solve a complex problem. When students have to debate ideas, reconcile conflicting perspectives, make sense of complicated content, stumble through complex ideas, and collectively work toward a solution, they are far more likely to be working at the limits of their communication skills than when they are delivering a prepared speech or presentation.

When it comes to problem-solving and taking on almost impossible problems, communication within teams is essential. A team's ability to communicate effectively can quickly become the limiting—or winning—factor in its success. In many collaborative classrooms, it's often not the teams with the students who think the quickest or even know the most content that are the most effective. Successful teams are often the ones who are able to communicate most effectively with one another.

To many educators' frustration and bemusement, it's common to witness teams where each student has a different piece of the puzzle, but collectively can't see the full picture. More often than not, this is because of the team's inability to communicate effectively.

On the other hand, teams filled with students with more developed communication skills—who ask good questions, restate and paraphrase ideas, and build off of one another's thinking—are able to outperform other teams even if their initial level of content knowledge or understanding may be lower.

Consequently, teachers must find ways to support the development of student communication skills in all aspects of the classroom experience, including the messiness of collaborative work.

Developing Informal Communication Skills

Teachers can develop students' informal communication skills using the same general approach they use to develop formal speaking skills. Instead of giving students an opportunity to develop a prepared speech or presentation, teachers can give students the opportunity to work together on a complex problem. Instead of providing students feedback on their prepared remarks and delivery, teachers can provide feedback on how students used their communications skills to work together. Instead of giving students additional opportunities to practice what they've learned in a series of speeches, teachers can provide multiple opportunities for students to practice communicating in small groups.

Consider the approach used by several teachers to help students develop their communication and collaboration skills while working in small groups, sometimes referred to as a "participation quiz" (Oakland Unified School District 2013). Informed by this approach, a teacher may start by providing a group-worthy task (something that actually invites and compels students to talk!) to his class. Rather than interrupting and intervening, the teacher simply walks around the room and observes. While observing, the teacher writes down specific phrases that he hears students say. After ten minutes or so, he captures thirty phrases, all direct quotes from students. He categorizes these phrases into three main categories he has chosen to emphasize and projects them onto a screen so that all of his students can see.

The first category of student phrases is "facilitation cues." These were phrases that students used that helped the group work effectively, such as, "Can someone read the task out loud?" "Does everyone understand?" and "Does anyone have any questions?" The teacher notices that some students are very good with facilitation cues, and others need much more practice and support. The difference in the quality of the facilitation has a huge impact on how effectively the group worked together and the progress they made on the task. The teacher realizes that it isn't a matter of some students wanting their group to run smoothly and others not; it is simply that some students know the language to make it happen while others have yet to figure it out.

The second category of student phrases is "questions," and the third category is "statements." Toward the end of class, the teacher brings the class back together and debriefs the phrases he heard. The teacher shares the facilitation cues and talks objectively about the impact they had on the group that used them. The teacher says, "When a member of group three said, 'Does anyone have any questions?' it gave her group the opportunity to check in with each other before diving into the task. This check-in surfaced a misunderstanding about what the task was about, which the group was able to reconcile before jumping in, which ended up saving the group a lot of time down the road."

The teacher is careful to be objective when he speaks about the language students used. Rather than saying that he likes a particular comment or question, he presents an objective observation, typically trying to connect the specific language used to the impact that the language had on the group. By talking objectively about the language, he tries to help students appreciate the impact effective communication can have on group performance.

The point is not for students to use particular language because the teacher wants them to use it. Rather, the point is for students to explore the impact communication has on how their group works together. In fact, students might come to realize that some of the most frustrating aspects of working in their team might be alleviated by changes to how they communicate with one another.

The teacher also spends time highlighting a few observations regarding the questions and the statements he heard. He points out that teams that asked more questions were able to develop solutions more quickly—a phenomenon that initially seems ironic to most students. Questions that were more specific were better understood by group members. Answers that contained the word "because" were particularly powerful because they often included a mathematical justification, not just an answer.

This entire debrief amounts to a five-minute investment of class time. The teacher conducts this feedback routine more frequently at the beginning of the year, or when he changes student groups, to help establish more effective norms from the onset. The teacher notices that these sorts of feedback routines support students to use facilitation cues, ask better questions, and provide stronger responses.

Perhaps one reason why interventions like these can produce positive change is that they create a virtuous cycle. When students start communicating more effectively, they experience firsthand the benefits of effective communication. They aren't using facilitation cues or asking better questions just because their teacher tells them to; they do it because it actually improves their experience.

Another reason why interventions like these can be effective is that the feedback and learning are grounded in students' own practice and experience. Talking about what makes effective communication is not an abstract conversation that is disconnected from the actual things students are doing. Quite the contrary, the support and feedback are embedded into students' in-the-moment experiences.

When interventions are embedded into the actual work of students—whether the interventions are targeted to support communication, collaboration, or culture—students begin to see these ideas as inherently tied to the academic work they do in class. Athletic coaches talk about effective communication and collaboration all of the time. Theater directors take great care to build a positive culture with their cast and crew. Consequently, it's not a stretch for students to see the connections between communication, collaboration, and culture and the success they experience on the playing field or on the theater stage. Teachers can make a similar commitment to helping students see the connection between these skills, their classroom experience, and the real work of professionals in their field, whether be it math, science, English, or any other subject matter.

Different Forms of Communication

Beyond communication in small teams, the types of communication required to take on complex problems take many forms across many different mediums. Skillful teachers can create experiences where students use email, social media, websites, and even video conferencing throughout the course of a task or project. Many of these mediums operate with different norms, and each can bring a different set of benefits and challenges. Too frequently, students experience these challenges outside the context of a supportive, low-risk, educational setting.

The submission of a job application or an inquiry to a college admissions officer may be the first time a student sends an email to an adult. The first time a student conducts a professional video conference could be for a job interview. Teachers have a great opportunity to use these tools to help students build skills and gain confidence in communicating across a variety of platforms to a variety of stakeholders, as they will likely be asked to do in whatever future role they assume.

Consider:

1. To what extent do students' learning experiences provide them with frequent opportunities to practice their communication?
2. What systems and routines can you develop to provide students with feedback so that they can improve their communication skills?
3. What constitutes effective communication in your discipline or subject area? How is it similar and different from other disciplines or subject areas? What supports can you provide to help students learn to communicate like a mathematician, or a scientist, or a historian, or a journalist, or an artist, or an engineer?
4. To what extent do students' learning experiences provide them with opportunities to practice communication across multiple channels, for multiple purposes, and for multiple audiences?

Chapter 10

Curiosity and Asking Good Questions

FOR THE PRESIDENT

Presidents aren't admired merely for what they know or can do. They are also admired for their ability to ask good questions of themselves, their team, the country, and the world. At times, questions can be more powerful than statements, and can precipitate critical dialogue and debate. To focus people's attention on an important problem, to help a community face a dilemma or conflict, or to inspire a team (or nation) to consider possible versions of the future, leaders often start by asking a question.

The ability to ask good questions requires a president to have genuine curiosity about the world, its people, its problems, and its opportunities. When a president is curious, they are more likely to be open to new ideas, explore the challenges of complex problems, and learn deeply. Ultimately, this can support a president's ability to envision future possibilities and create solutions never before imagined. Furthermore, modeling curiosity and asking good questions can inspire others to do the same.

IN THE CLASSROOM

For students to gain those same skills, curiosity, wonderment, and imagination must be nurtured. Teachers have an important role to play, as they can help students explore exciting connections across disciplines and pursue answers to their own driving questions.

Unfortunately, school can have an adverse impact on our students' curiosity. Rather than a place where young people go to explore, discover, and ask questions, school can be a place where students are asked to consume, digest, and regurgitate. Many classrooms hold no time or space for student curiosity. Educational researcher and author Tony Wagner (2012) argues, "We are all born curious, creative, and imaginative. And the best schools—from pre-K to graduate school—continue to develop these capabilities in students." Instead of seeing curiosity as something our students are expected to practice outside of school, how can we make school a place where curiosity blossoms?

Consider how curiosity can take form for students outside of school. While standing in line at a restaurant, a group of teenagers examine a very large gumball machine in the restaurant's lobby. One of them ponders out loud, "I wonder how often they have to refill this machine."

What an interesting question! The question is far more compelling than the classic "guess how many gumballs are in this machine" prompt. Unlike the classic question, this individual's question requires us to consider several more variables that are far less certain: how frequently do people buy gumballs from this machine, what's the capacity of the machine and what's the current level, and how low does the gumball supply need to get before it makes sense to refill it?

This individual's question offers an inspirational model for the types of questions we could be posing to our students. The question was simply stated but not easily answered. Everyone knew what the individual was asking, but no one would have an immediate answer, or even an immediate strategy to begin thinking about it.

Additionally, this problem invites the use of a wide range of mathematical tools, from highly sophisticated to relatively simple. For example, you could explore this problem by looking at how the height of the gumball level within the glass globe changes at different rates when the container is 90 percent full compared to 50 percent full. Alternatively, you could explore the situation using relatively simple formulas, such as the formula for the volume of a sphere.

It's likely that most people could contribute some insight or knowledge to the problem-solving process, but it's also true that the task could inspire quite sophisticated and complex thinking and problem-solving, particularly when a group might work on the problem together.

Beyond the fascinating question from this individual, there's another important question to ask, How frequently is this individual given opportunities to ask similarly interesting and rich questions at school? Was he aware of the connections between the question he asked and the concepts he was learning about in his math class? Did he see how the ideas he was learning in class could be used to explore the very question he just posed? Or, was the chasm between school and the "real world" so great that he couldn't possibly imagine any connection?

Humans are naturally curious. We naturally generate interesting questions and seek deep understanding—just ask any kindergarten teacher or parent. As humans, we are constantly trying to make sense of our world.

However, this outward expression of curiosity too often dwindles as students make their way through the formal education system. It's painful to acknowledge that we as educators might be part of the problem, but it very well may be the case.

Jo Boaler, a mathematics educator and professor at Stanford University, argues that a narrow focus on performance and speed in the math classroom gives students the wrong idea about what math is actually about and can turn students off to the entire subject. As Boaler (2017) argues, "The performance culture of mathematics has destroyed a vibrant, essential subject for so many people. As schools have worked to encourage a few speedy calculators, they've neglected to teach the kind of creative, quantitative thinking that can open new worlds."

It's not a stretch to say that the educational experience in many classrooms can be described in the following way: *Teachers ask students questions to which the teachers already know the answers.* Nothing could be further from an authentic inquiry experience, and students know it. School can be quickly reduced to a guessing game between teachers and students, where students are rewarded for reproducing the correct answers that teachers already have in their heads. This is not an environment that is likely to spur genuine curiosity. In fact, it is far more likely to squash it.

Now consider Sasha, a teacher who poses the teenager's gumball machine question to her students. What's the difference between this question and the kinds of questions teachers typically ask? Sasha genuinely doesn't know the answer. She is now in the same learning stance as her students. The advantage she has, however, is that she is well versed in problem-solving and using mathematics to think about and solve interesting problems. Now, rather than being the owner of "the right answer," she's a coach that helps students develop their ability to use mathematics to think about these sorts of problems. Sasha's role shifts; now her job is to help students develop their ability to think like a mathematician.

This is a far more authentic experience because Sasha doesn't have to play coy and pretend she doesn't have the correct answer. She places herself alongside her students as a problem solver and explorer, and her students get to see what "doing mathematics" actually looks and feels like.

Now, consider how Sasha could go even a step further. Instead of generating the question herself, she sources possible questions from her class. Showing her class a photo of the gumball machine, she may ask her students what questions they have. Her class discusses and debates which questions are the most interesting and compelling. Perhaps they break up into small teams, each team taking on the question that is most exciting to them.

While Sasha is unlikely to know the answers to any of the questions the groups are pursuing, she can still support the entire class by helping students break down the problem like mathematicians. When students have the experience of using mathematics to answer a question that they themselves have generated, a question for which there is no answer in the back of the book, there is the potential for students' relationships with mathematics to undergo a powerful shift. Now, mathematics is a discipline that can be used to think about and make sense of the world around them. They can be empowered by mathematics. Mathematics can support their curiosity. As Boaler (2017) writes, "If we encourage new generations of students who love learning and love math, we'll raise up kids who are prepared to take their place in society as free, empowered thinkers."

While the example here is one from mathematics, the same general ideas extend to other disciplines as well. Whether asking a question about a historical event, a physical phenomenon, or the true intentions of a character in a novel, teachers have the ability to sit alongside their students, collectively exploring a question to which no one has an answer (yet).

Rather than prodding students toward an answer that is already in the back of a book, teachers can empower students with the tools of their disciplines— to think, question, and act like a mathematician, a historian, a scientist, an engineer, or a literary analyst—to make sense of a compelling question and pursue an answer. In doing so, students are far more likely to see and explore other questions outside of school, further developing their curiosity.

If you're looking for a quick assessment of how authentic a classroom task is, it might be helpful to consider the *truthful* teacher response to the classic student question, "Teacher, how do I do this?" In many classrooms, the teacher, almost as if citing a line from a script, will say, "I don't know, what do you think?" The intention is good; the teacher is trying to redirect the question and push the student's thinking.

However, frequently the "I don't know, what do you think?" response is also a lie. That's because, the vast majority of the time, the teacher actually does know the answer to the student's question. The teacher wrote the problem herself, along with the answer key. Everyone—the teacher and the student—knows this, and most of the time everyone is just playing along. As Alfie Kohn (1999, 56) argues, "The discussions teachers conduct are often fishing expeditions: they're not invitations to reflect deeply on complicated issues but attempts to elicit the right answer." Again, teachers give students problems to which the teachers already know the answers.

Imagine the alternative. Imagine what would happen if the teacher asked a question to which she really doesn't know the answer. Now, in response to the student's question, she could reply, "I don't know . . . let's figure it out together!"

Thinking about and working through real problems is far more likely to cultivate your curiosity than trying to see if you can determine the same answer as someone else already has.

In life, we tend to learn new things when we have to. When we come across a word we don't know, we look it up in a dictionary. Most of us don't look up random words, thinking that we may, one day, come across them.

As absurd as that sounds, plenty of students' experiences in school could be described in this way. First, students learn some subject-area knowledge. Then, they are asked to apply it. However, this order can be flipped. We can nurture student curiosity by creating situations in which students want to learn more. Consider the problem, question, conflict, or dilemma that would require students to ask interesting questions and pursue worthwhile knowledge. Teachers can expose students to problems first, and then help them discover the knowledge or concepts that will help them make sense of them and pursue solutions.

When students have opportunities to express their curiosity in school, they are far more likely to be curious outside of school.

We want our leaders to be curious individuals because curiosity leads to continuous learning, deeper exploration of complicated ideas, and leaning into unknown territory—all essential elements for taking on almost impossible problems.

Consider:

1. What opportunities do students have to generate and explore their own questions? What support can you provide to help them with question generation and exploration?
2. What problems, questions, conflicts, or dilemmas can you create that are likely to generate student curiosity? How will this curiosity lead to rich and deep learning experiences?

Chapter 11

Resilience

FOR THE PRESIDENT

The frequency with which a president makes mistakes or encounters setbacks requires an unusual tolerance for the risk of failure. It's instructive to remember that Abraham Lincoln lost several nominations and elections before becoming the president. What if he had quit after any one of those defeats? How many of us could tolerate that many personal losses before throwing in the towel? How many of us would be hesitant to start, simply to avoid the possibility of failure altogether?

We generally have high expectations for our leaders. As our expectations increase, so too does the likelihood that not all of our hopes and dreams will be met. One way to limit the risk of failure is to only strive for safe and modest goals. However, this is the exact opposite of what we expect of our president and hope for ourselves—a willingness and ability to take on almost impossible problems. Therefore, a president must be resilient.

IN THE CLASSROOM

High-performing people tend to have a special relationship with failure. A failure must sting enough to ensure that they learn from the experience, but it can't be so painful that ambitious goals are avoided altogether. Some individuals can be motivated by failure. Rather than failure forcing them to stop, it influences them to dig deeper.

The ability to keep going in the face of failure and setbacks is widely seen as an important aspect of leadership. Resilience is bolstered by a clear sense of purpose and a worthwhile aim. We are willing to bear more failure and justify more risk when we pursue something that we believe to be important. We don't tend to make sacrifices for things we find meaningless.

While school is not the only venue in which students can develop and pursue their passions, it certainly ought to do a better job for more students than it currently does.

Many educators complain of students who fail to demonstrate grit, resilience, and a go-getter attitude, while simultaneously giving them work that is routine, mundane, and void of meaning. Most adults have a low tolerance for busy work. If we were to assess our ability to stick with problems and bounce back from failures, and the only evidence we gathered on ourselves was when we engaged in dull work given to us by others, we would probably have a similarly grim assessment of ourselves.

At times, educators can be guilty of focusing too much on a symptom, rather than addressing the underlying problem. Instead of designing experiences that are more likely to engender intrinsic motivation and a sense of purpose and meaning, we sometimes employ elaborate systems built on extrinsic forms of motivation in our attempts to get students committed and engaged. However, as Tony Wagner argues, this approach isn't always the best way to help students pursue their goals. Wagner (2012) writes, "It is this combination of play, passion, and purpose—rather than the carrot-and-stick motivation of most classrooms—that best develops the discipline and perseverance required to be a successful innovator."

Educators can help students develop resilience by helping them develop and pursue their passions. While it may not be possible, or even desirable, for the work of school to be fully determined by the passions and interests of individual students, there's no excuse for school to be a place entirely void of it.

Educators can also help students develop resilience by sharing their own stories. Angela Duckworth is a psychologist at the University of Pennsylvania who focuses on the development of character strengths such as kindness, purpose, curiosity, and grit. Duckworth uses her own experiences to help demystify the pursuit of passion. In a 2017 interview with *Forbes*, Duckworth (2017) explains, "I spend a lot of time with young people, and I do my best to model for them both passion and perseverance. I'm very open about how hard I work and how committed I am, how I am always, always trying to do just one thing better than I did yesterday, and yes, how devastated I feel when I fail and how, no matter what, I eventually dry my tears and get up again."

When students have more experiences doggedly pursuing their passions, the discipline and resilience they develop can be transferred to other pursuits. Unfortunately, for many students, school does not provide much support to students in developing and pursuing passions.

What if school provided more outlets for students to explore their own interests and then supported them as they take on ambitious goals? That's precisely what some students experience through extracurricular activities such as athletics, drama, and other clubs. While these spaces can be powerful venues for some students to build their resiliency, these opportunities aren't always available for all students and may not resonate with others. Furthermore, opportunities to develop and nurture passion don't have to be limited to extracurricular experiences. Teachers can create opportunities for students to explore their passions through the types of learning tasks they create and the experiences they design.

Developing resilience is about more than just developing and pursuing passion. Students need strong and supportive relationships with adults. According to the Center on the Developing Child at Harvard University, "The single most common factor for children who develop resilience is at least one stable and committed relationship with a supportive parent, caregiver, or other adult" (Center on the Developing Child, n.d.). Seeing as though children spend a significant portion of their waking hours in school, educators have a critical role in forming the types of strong and supportive relationships that are connected with the development of resilience.

Furthermore, when students build a sense of self-efficacy and perceived control, they are building positive influences that can optimize resilience, according to the Center on the Developing Child at Harvard University. Building student self-efficacy and perceived control can be pursued by the careful and intentional design of learning experiences, as explored throughout this book.

Taking on almost impossible problems will require resilient individuals with a healthy track record of sticking with problems over extended periods of time. Schools can create opportunities for more students to have those types of experiences.

Consider:

1. What patterns do you see between student resilience and the type of work with which students engage? Are students engaging in learning experiences that are worth their resilience?
2. What do you know about your students' passions? What opportunities do you have to coach, encourage, and support them as they pursue them?
3. What are you doing to form strong and supportive relationships with students, particularly those who may have had, or are having, adverse experiences?

Section Two

TRANSFORMING THE CLASSROOM

Most teachers have aspirational visions for their classrooms. These visions frequently entail students working collaboratively to solve rich and meaningful tasks that leverage their creativity; foster their curiosity; and test their leadership, communication, and critical thinking skills. However, even for teachers who explicitly state these goals, most classrooms fall short of these aspirational visions.

Why?

In spite of seismic shifts in the world that surrounds our classrooms, little has changed in terms of how students experience these formal learning environments. Most students experience school more or less the same way their counterparts did decades ago.

When teachers are asked, "What goals do you have for your students?" the responses seem remarkably consistent across grade levels, disciplines, and schools. Teachers can be quick to espouse the aspirational goals they have for their students. More often than not, teachers will list a set of things that check off the skills and mind-sets that are outlined in the first section of this book. Teachers will say they value collaboration, creativity, student voice, and leadership. They want their students to have agency, care about one another, and think deeply. They want their students to be lifelong learners and meaningful contributors to their communities. They want their students to love learning.

But there must be a second part to this question. "How are these values reflected in the daily experience of your classroom?" When teachers are asked to describe the *specific* ways in which their values are manifested in their daily practice, their answers can be less clear. Too much time is spent in too many of our classrooms doing things that are neutral to our goals at best and in opposition to our goals at worst.

We say we want our students to be collaborative, but we rarely give them opportunities to do anything beyond share their answers with their partner.

We say we want students to think critically, but we only ask questions to which we are expecting a specific answer.

We say we want students to love learning, but all of the classroom stakes are oriented around a single-letter grade.

We can also be quick to identify the things that are holding us back. Frequently mentioned as the culprits of this disconnect are factors outside a teacher's control: her district-mandated curriculum, his lack of time, or the upcoming standardized test. These factors are real and most certainly have an impact on the type of learning experiences educators are able to create for their students. Without a doubt, those who have decision-making authority regarding the policy and structural issues that influence the learning that happens within classrooms must take their job seriously and thoughtfully consider the consequences of their decisions.

However, in most situations, there still exists a great deal of innovative potential that we as educators have yet to realize. For many of our classrooms, we will need to fully realize that innovative potential if we are to create the types of learning environments capable of equipping students to take on almost impossible problems.

In this section, we'll explore a shift in how we can conceptualize our work as educators. Rather than seeing our work as that of instructors, coaches, or even facilitators, we will explore the benefit of viewing our work as that of *designers*.

In the final section, we'll explore the challenge of change and why doing things differently is difficult, even when we ourselves want the change to happen. We will also explore ideas as to how teachers can stay renewed and energized through it all and find pleasure and meaning in their work.

Chapter 12

Designing a Learning Environment

Over one hundred years ago, John Dewey (1916) wrote, "We never educate directly, but indirectly by means of the environment. Whether we permit chance environments to do the work, or whether we design environments for the purpose makes a great difference." Rather than simply being deliverers of content or facilitators of process, what if educators embraced a broader conception of their role: designers of learning environments? What new possibilities would this conception allow educators to see, and how might it influence the choices they make?

Viewing the role of an educator as a *designer of learning environments* can make teaching far more exciting as well as far more complex. The framing forces teachers to consider the sort of environmental experiences that are most likely to lead to the desired learning goals. Rather than taking so many elements of our current classrooms as given, it forces us to consider the full experience students have and make honest assessments on whether those experiences actually align with the goals we have for our students.

For example, if we want our students to develop as leaders, does an environment where they spend most of their time silently seated in rows make any sense?

If we want our students to develop as communicators, who should be doing most of the talking?

If we want our students to become creative and collaborative problem solvers, will routine worksheets with single correct answers and individual assessments achieve that purpose?

The environment in which students find themselves will have a profound effect on what they will do and how they will learn. One group of professionals that knows this reality well is playground designers. While we might not initially see playgrounds as intentional learning environments, they share many of the same goals as highly engaging classrooms.

The best playgrounds inspire curiosity, promote exploration, support safe risk-taking, and are inherently engaging. They are able to do this, somewhat ingeniously, without the support of a teacher telling students what to do and how to use the space. In fact, playgrounds can get students to explore, play, take risks, and learn, all without motivating students with grades! This all happens through the *means of the environment*, an environment that was carefully designed for specific purposes.

Form follows function. Educators must get super clear on the function they want their classroom environments to serve. Do you want your classroom to develop creativity? Or perhaps you want to focus on cultivating empathy and curiosity? If so, what form should your classroom take in order to achieve that function? Just like a playground designed to develop upper arm strength and risk-taking would look different than a playground designed to promote balance and safety, a classroom must be intentionally designed with its goals in mind.

It can be hard to think of the classroom environment being something that educators can intentionally "design." Perhaps this is because too many of the design elements are so ingrained in tradition and expectation that we fail to notice them anymore.

Consider the standard lesson plan template for a math classroom: (1) opening problem, (2) review the homework, (3) lecture on new content, and (4) individual practice. This template is so frequently used that we might not see it as an actual design choice. Instead, this template is where a teacher *starts* to plan. Rather than zooming out and starting our design from scratch, we design within the constraints and boundaries of this narrow template.

Furthermore, consider the physical space of the environment. While we might not initially consider the location of a class as a design choice, perhaps there are times when it makes sense for a math class to meet in an auditorium, a science class to meet in a gymnasium, and a history class to meet at the local city hall.

It's astounding how many things we take as given when it comes to the design of our formal learning environments. Does this mean we are necessarily lazy or unthoughtful? Of course not. Taking most of these design choices for granted allows us to focus on the smaller number of elements that we think are the most important, and the ones we are most likely to modify based on our objective. This is completely reasonable. Most of the time it's probably better for a teacher to think about what opening problem she will prepare for her class than to think, "Where will my class meet today?" However, she should at least consider, in the back of her mind, that classroom location is indeed a design choice, and she may choose to alter it every once in a while, depending on her goals.

Consider:

1. What are the aspirational goals you have for your classroom? In what ways is the form of your classroom aligned, or misaligned, with those goals?
2. What are some of the critical design elements of your classroom? Which elements might be ready for your reexamination, based on the goals you are trying to achieve?

Chapter 13

Classrooms as Organizations

When designing their learning environments, it may be helpful for teachers to think about their classrooms as organizations. Broadly defined, organizations are groups of people organized together to achieve certain goals. This broad definition nicely describes a classroom: students and teachers work together to learn and grow.

We know that different organizations are designed to achieve different goals, so how an organization chooses to organize itself matters a great deal. We also know that some organizations are highly effective at achieving their goals, while others are less so. It's important, then, to consider the organization of a classroom and its effectiveness at achieving its goals.

Harvard Business School professors Clayton Christensen and Stephen Kaufman have studied organizational capabilities—that is, what an organization is able to achieve. Some of us may have experience as members of highly effective and efficient organizations, where ambitious goals are achieved on a regular basis and where the culture and high levels of trust make us feel like we belong.

Some of us may also have experiences with highly dysfunctional organizations, where nothing seems to ever get done and people resent the time they spend together. The same wide spectrum exists for classrooms. Consequently, it's worth our time to explore the foundational elements of an organization, to see what we can learn to inform changes to our classrooms.

Preparing students to take on almost impossible problems will require remarkably powerful learning environments. As a result, most of us need to think carefully about how we can work to develop the capabilities of our classroom organizations. Teachers can use Christensen and Kaufman's framework to think about the different design elements of their classroom, and what changes they can make to build their classroom's capabilities.

Christensen and Kaufman (2006) argue that what an organization is able to achieve is the result of three sets of factors: priorities, resources, and processes.

PRIORITIES

To understand why an organization achieves what it does, you need to first understand its priorities. While most teachers can readily recite on command their most virtuous priorities, making meaningful change to your classroom may require a deeper, more personal, investigation.

Our espoused priorities are typically the ones we are most eager to discuss and most proud to share. These are the priorities we are likely to put up on our classroom walls, share with our students and families, and discuss with our colleagues. These priorities may include elements such as being responsive to individual student needs, creating an inclusive classroom environment for all learners, never giving up on a student, and creating learning tasks and assessments that match the love and appreciation we have for our disciplines.

However, beyond the priorities that we are eager to share, inevitably, there are others. While these other priorities may not take center stage in our minds, they still may play leading roles in terms of their impact on our teaching and what happens in our classrooms.

While a teacher may have a genuine priority to provide individual feedback to his students, he may also have a real and legitimate priority for spending time with his own children when he returns home from work. While these priorities are not always mutually exclusive, there may be times when they come into direct conflict with one another.

These other priorities—at times competing priorities—can create a significant barrier for our attempts to change. A broader discussion of this dynamic will take place in the next section regarding the challenge of change. For now, it's important to at least recognize the complex, and sometimes competing, set of priorities that we have as professionals and real people. To fully understand and appreciate how priorities affect our organization's (classroom's) capabilities, we need to consider all of our priorities, not just the ones we would be happy to put on a bumper sticker.

The easiest way to surface these other priorities is to simply look at our actions. During the times when you are not fully expressing your most "virtuous" priorities, what priorities are likely influencing your behavior and decisions? Using your actions and decisions as evidence, try to map them back to your priorities.

Getting a clear picture of your priorities is important because your priorities create a lens through which you see some opportunities and fail to see others. For example, if a teacher has a priority of elevating diverse student voices, she is more likely to identify moments in her teaching to create space for students to share alternative points of view. These opportunities may remain completely hidden from a teacher who doesn't hold that same priority.

Even if a teacher truly values diverse student voices, she may also have another priority—one that is less obvious to her—to avoid conflict. This may be a personal preference influenced by her own personality, or it may stem from a lack of confidence in her ability to effectively facilitate a classroom discussion that gets contentious. By recognizing that she also has a priority to avoid conflict, the teacher can understand why she may avoid opportunities to bring in diverse perspectives, even when she says she values doing so.

Consider:

1. What are your top priorities for yourself, your classroom, and/or your school? To get the full complicated picture, don't be afraid to list priorities that may come in conflict with each other.
2. What opportunities do these priorities help you see, and what opportunities are you likely to miss?

RESOURCES

The second element that determines an organization's capabilities is its resources. While classroom resources generally refer to physical objects, such as books, tools, furniture, and supplies, there are many other types of resources a teacher must consider.

There are human resources in the knowledge, perspectives, backgrounds, and creativity of the members of the classroom. When it comes to engaging in a thoughtful discussion about a novel, debating a recent political event, or working through a challenging math problem, the knowledge and perspectives that individual students bring to the table can represent incredibly valuable resources.

There are also social resources embedded within the ability of individuals to coordinate, cooperate, collaborate, and work together to solve problems. At times, these social resources can actually create capabilities that extend beyond the sum of the capabilities of the individuals, when class members are able to build upon each other's thinking to create new knowledge, ideas, and creative insights.

According to Christensen and Kaufman's organizational capabilities theory, whether and how these resources are brought to bear will influence the capabilities of the classroom. Clearly, a classroom that fully leverages the individual creativity and collaborative problem-solving capabilities of all its members will be able to achieve things that go above and beyond what a classroom that fails to leverage those resources would be able to.

Seeing a classroom as resource-rich, regardless of the tangible resources available, may be the first step in unlocking serious capabilities. In order to leverage these resources, a teacher must be able to identify them. We see resources through the lens of our priorities, so what we prioritize will have a significant impact on what we see. For example, a teacher who prioritizes collaboration is far more likely to see his student's collaborative abilities, or collaborative potential, as a resource compared to a teacher who only prioritizes individual achievement.

Uncovering previously hidden resources may require teachers to revisit and interrogate their set of priorities.

Consider:

1. What are your classroom's, school's, and/or community's greatest resources? Which of these resources are being leveraged, and which are not?
2. How are your priorities influencing what resources you are able to see? If you were to broaden, narrow, or shift your priorities, what new resources might you see?

PROCESSES

In organizations, processes transform resources into things of greater value. The previous section referred to the idea of "leveraging resources." A resource is leveraged when there is a process that takes advantage of the potential value of the resource. Without a process, resources can have little or no impact on your classroom's capabilities.

Consider the example of the teacher who values diverse student voices. This priority helps her identify an incredible resource in her classroom: the diverse experiences, perspectives, and values of her students. The mere presence of this resource does not guarantee that it will actually have any positive impact on the classroom's capabilities. The resource is there, but it's up to the teacher to find a way to help the class benefit from it.

The teacher must design and utilize a process to transform the resource into something of greater value. For example, the teacher may engage the class in the process of a skillfully facilitated large group discussion. During the process of this discussion, the teacher calls upon students to voice diverse perspectives, compare and contrast ideas, make connections and distinctions, and restate the ideas of other students. This process has the effect of transforming a classroom resource (student's diverse perspectives) into something of greater value (a robust conversation that helps students appreciate the complexity of the topic of discussion).

Being skillful and intentional about designing and implementing thoughtful classroom processes is where many teachers fall short. There are too many archetypal examples to list here, but mentioning a few might help make the point.

Consider the teacher who sees student creativity as a resource but never designs any learning activities that actually call upon students to use their creativity.

Imagine the teacher who always claims that students should be resources for each other but the vast majority of classroom tasks and assessments are conducted individually, and even when students do work collaboratively, they are given no support to do so effectively.

Finally, consider the teacher who knows that students' knowledge and perspectives could be valuable resources for each other but doesn't design a process for students to share feedback with each other.

Designing processes to leverage resources doesn't have to be overly complicated or sophisticated. For example, consider the college professor who saw students' sense of humor as a resource for the classroom. To leverage this resource, he created a process whereby each class would start with a student telling a joke in front of the class. Had it not been for this intentionally designed process, it's quite possible that this resource would have gone underutilized.

Creating powerful learning environments that help students develop the knowledge, skills, and mind-sets needed to take on almost impossible problems will require highly capable classrooms. Supporting students to become effective collaborators; engaging students in deep and critical thinking; nurturing student curiosity, resilience, humility, and confidence; and building an inclusive classroom that instills a sense of justice and caring for all reflect a classroom with truly awesome capabilities.

A classroom environment capable of these things won't emerge without intentional and deliberate design. With their ultimate goals in mind, teachers can consider how the priorities, resources, and processes of their classrooms come together to create these powerful capabilities.

Consider:

1. What are the processes that your classroom and/or school relies on the most? Are these processes effective at leveraging your classroom's resources?

2. What new processes may need to be designed and implemented to fully take advantage of other, previously underutilized, resources?

CLASSROOM DESIGN—A CASE STUDY

As designers of learning environments, committed to creating classroom organizations powerful enough to match the ambitious goals we have for our students, we as educators must consider how priorities, resources, and processes come together to create something powerful and special. Teachers must be clear on the priorities that will drive their design. Teachers must identify resources that will help bring to life their priorities, and teachers must create processes to fully leverage those resources.

Consider the following example to see how teachers can use these three elements to design more powerful and effective learning environments capable of equipping students with the knowledge, skills, and mind-sets to take on almost impossible problems.

Imagine Rachel, a teacher who is desperate to infuse more energy into her unit on the Civil War. In spite of the fact that she finds the Civil War significant and compelling, her students never seem to share the same zeal for digging in and trying to figure out what exactly happened and why.

As a teacher, she desperately wants her students to love history and be skillful consumers of the historical documents they review. She wants her students to develop their critical thinking skills, to be curious and ask good questions, and to communicate their thinking effectively. Indeed, helping her students think and act like real historians is a significant priority for her as an educator.

Furthermore, Rachel wants her students to feel more empowered as learners and take more initiative in class. Rachel sometimes feels that she is the one doing all of the hard work and heavy lifting, and students are simply along for the ride. She knows that preparing students to take on almost impossible problems will require her students to develop their skills in leadership, collaboration, and initiative. As an educator, she wants students to develop these skills as a result of her class and not in spite of it.

Upon reflection, Rachel also uncovers that she has another priority that may be influencing the types of experiences she designs for her students. Like many of us, she also has a (somewhat hidden) priority for control and order. She starts to realize that this priority has influenced her Civil War unit in a rather particular way. Rachel's desire for control and order has translated into this unit becoming a series of lectures about the Civil War.

Ironically, Rachel's approach is in direct conflict with her other priorities for her students to think and act like real historians, to be curious, and to communicate with each other. Developing a more complete picture of her priorities by recognizing how some of them may be in conflict with others is an important first step in allowing her to rethink what might be possible.

We identify resources through the lens of our priorities. Consequently, Rachel's priority to support her budding historians focuses her attention toward the resources required to help students think and act like real historians. Since real historians often work with primary source documents, she identifies a set of four documents, each with an interesting, and different, account of what happened during a significant event during the Civil War. She also recognizes that historians construct arguments about the past and often discuss and debate with one another. Recognizing this priority allows her to see another resource in the room that she hasn't previously considered—the students themselves! Her students are always debating and arguing.

These newly identified resources—the primary source documents and the students' interest and ability to argue and debate with one another—create the potential for something powerful. However, the mere existence of these resources is not enough. Every day, in every classroom, resources go untapped and underutilized. Thoughtful teachers must design thoughtful processes to help ensure that the class benefits from the resources.

Spending time thinking about what processes she needs resurfaces Rachel's other priority—her priority for control and order. She begins to remember previous units where she attempted to do something more ambitious and how things went terribly wrong. Early in her career, she gave small teams a packet of primary source documents and had them prepare for a mock trial. The results were disastrous, to say the least.

While some groups managed to create the beginnings of a thoughtful argument, most groups engaged in little to no meaningful analysis of the primary source documents. In some of the groups, a single individual did most or all of the work. Furthermore, some groups appeared to be plagued by interpersonal conflict, which was particularly troubling because it seemed to have the effect of further isolating a few students who she was already struggling to meaningfully engage.

While the mock trial was amusing, there was very little evidence that much had happened in terms of historical thinking or deep analysis.

Furthermore, students didn't seem particularly curious about uncovering what actually happened; they were simply walking through the steps to finish an assignment. Rachel also vividly recalls the moment when her department chair entered the classroom during "work time" when nearly half of her students were playing on their cellphones and the embarrassment she felt.

While Rachel tended to see herself as a competent teacher who engaged her students in rich and meaningful work, she felt the complete opposite that day. In fact, that moment threatened the very way she saw herself as a professional. That was the last time she had attempted to do anything other than lecture. As Rachel considers all of the things that went wrong the last time, the series of lectures begins to look more and more attractive once again.

Then comes an epiphany. Rachel's other priority is not *control* or *order*. It is *effectiveness* and *meaning*. Her previous experience wasn't negative because she wasn't in control or the classroom felt out of order—it was negative because it did not achieve her goals to help students think and act like historians. This epiphany helps her reframe her design challenge. Having the raw resources available isn't enough. She needs to create thoughtful processes to ensure that the classroom benefits from those resources.

Rachel begins to consider each resource, and what process might be needed to ensure that the resource is actually leveraged. She starts with her set of primary source documents. She realizes that simply giving students a stack of documents will not lead to rich historical analysis. She recognizes that students need help to understand how they should approach their analysis. Consequently, she identifies some tools and graphic organizers that help students consider the source of the document, the author, their purpose, and the context within which the document was created. She creates a series of reflection questions that helps guide students through a thoughtful analysis of the document. She designs a mini-lecture that introduces these tools and even models the practice in front of the entire class.

She also develops a rubric, aligned with these additional resources, that helps articulate the components of a strong historical argument. She builds time into her lessons to have students practice using the rubric to assess contemporary arguments she gets from current news stories.

She also realizes that students need additional support to ensure that they benefit from the other resource in their classroom—one another. While Rachel knows that all of her students have important insights and perspectives to share, previous attempts at group work have mostly resulted in only a small handful of students making meaningful contributions. Again, this is a classic case of resources going untapped and underutilized.

To help ensure that her students fully benefit from one another, she starts to think about the processes she will need to design to help facilitate effective collaboration. She decides to create a group "norming" process, which she will facilitate on the first day of the unit. The process follows a strict protocol that ensures every group member speaks, that explicit norms and working agreements are discussed and agreed upon, and that everyone signs a "group contract."

After consulting with a colleague who frequently uses group work, Rachel borrows another protocol that supports teams to reflect on their collaboration. She plans to reserve the final five minutes of each class period for students to engage in this reflection protocol, where team members identify what is going well, what they hope to change, and tangible action steps to move forward. Teams document the responses to these questions and share them with Rachel.

She feels particularly excited by this team reflection protocol because her previous adventure into collaborative learning left her feeling confused and unsure about what was actually happening within each group. This new process gives Rachel valuable insight into how each group is progressing, which allows her to determine the types of supports and interventions that she may need to provide.

Furthermore, she's hopeful that the team reflection protocol will also help support some of her other goals—to build student initiative and leadership skills. Rather than simply wishing students demonstrated more ownership over their learning process, she feels excited that she is actually doing something to support them in doing so.

Rachel also creates a participation tracker for herself to use. Similar to the communication feedback routine described in chapter 9 of this book, she plans to closely monitor groups as they work, and track different comments, questions, and facilitation cues that students use while working together. She can use these comments to provide direct feedback to the groups and the class as a whole to help ensure that their collaboration is getting stronger as the unit progresses. Given the previous challenges Rachel has encountered with collaboration in the past, she is particularly interested in how equitable the participation is within groups. It appears as though students for whom English is not their first language talk less than their peers, and so she plans to pay particularly close attention to participation patterns.

Additionally, other factors, such as the race and gender of her students, appear to have an impact on who speaks, who is listened to, and whose ideas are adopted by the group. Students also seem to have different expectations of each other, appearing to believe that some students are "smart" and have a lot to contribute, while others aren't and don't.

These disturbing patterns in how her students have worked together in the past have tempered her initial enthusiasm for having students work together again. These previous experiences could also be the genesis of her supposed priorities for control and order. However, now that she has a clear process to monitor student groups, gather data, provide feedback, and intervene when necessary, she is much more confident in her ability to help support effective collaboration.

Rachel also creates a comprehensive timeline for the week during which the project is to occur, which outlines key benchmarks and formative assessments along the way. She even builds an opportunity, half way through the unit, for pairs of teams to present their emerging ideas with each other and then provide each other feedback based on the rubric. Rachel is excited by this opportunity because it gives students additional practice and exposure with the rubric, offers her more visibility into the progress of each group, provides an opportunity for students to strengthen their work, requires students to practice and develop their communication skills, and delegates more responsibility to her students—all things she cares deeply about!

Finally, she creates more structure for the final performance assessment. Rather than a mock trial, which was fun but not fully authentic, given the context, she decides that the final assessment will be a mock presidential cabinet meeting that takes place within President Lincoln's office. Each student will be assigned a role (e.g., president, secretary of state, secretary of war). The meeting will last fifteen minutes, during which time the group will discuss what they should do and why they should do it.

Rachel recalls that her previous mock trial attempt didn't allow her to get a clear picture into what *individual* students learned from the experience. It was difficult to parse out the individual contributions and learning from the group performance. Consequently, she decides to create an additional assessment process and will require each student to submit an individual paper in which they construct their own historical arguments based on their research.

Because of time constraints, she'll need each group to have their cabinet meeting at the same time, so she decides to have each group video record their conversation with a cell phone, for her to review later. She realizes that the recording process presents an additional opportunity for self-assessment. She decides to have students review their own recording and assess their team's performance using their rubric, along with a reflection.

While Rachel is excited by what she has designed, she's also exhausted. Will all this work be worth it? After all, she's replacing three days of lectures with a week-long project. But what happens the following week? Does it actually make sense to invest so much of her planning time into a single project that only lasts a week?

Plenty of teachers have been in Rachel's shoes and have asked similar questions. Is this significant investment of time and energy into a single lesson or a single project actually worth it? There are at least three things that should calm Rachel's concerns.

First, Rachel is not just developing a unit; she's developing her classroom's capabilities. By deeply exploring her priorities, resources, and processes, she's actively investing in changes to her classroom that will pay dividends far beyond one particular moment in time. The next time she attempts to do something similar, she will be building off of the groundwork that this initial experience created. Through this experience, she's developing her skills as a designer. She's exploring the impact that changes to her classroom design have on the experiences of her students. In the future, she'll be able to make sharper and smarter decisions based on what she has learned from previous designs. In short, it's not just about developing this unit—it's about using this unit to *develop herself* as a professional.

Second, a truly rich experience, even if it only occurs once in a while, is better than nothing. When prompted to think about what we remember from our own experiences in school, many of us tend to recall a specific unit, lesson, or project. Even if it occurred decades ago, it might still have a profound effect on us. This is an awesome (and daunting) reality for us as educators. The experiences we create for our students matter, and so making those experiences rich and meaningful—to the extent possible—is important.

However, the impact of that one lesson, unit, or project on students may not be isolated to that one particular moment in time. For instance, after Rachel's students experience their presidential cabinet meeting, they may change how they approach primary source documents. They may be more attentive to how information is consumed, analyzed, and used. They may ask deeper questions and consider the profound consequences of how we make sense of information. They may be more curious about our world and how those in power make decisions.

In other words, students may be building their own capacity to take on almost impossible problems. Consequently, this experience can help transform future experiences, even ones that are less flashy and less ambitious.

Finally, while Rachel has signed up for a lot of work, it's substantively different than the kind of work that she spends most of her time doing. People don't tend to get burned out simply because they work too hard; they get burned out because their work lacks challenge, meaning, or purpose.

As we will discuss in the upcoming chapter on teacher flourishing, engaging in these sorts of professional challenges may very well be what sustains Rachel as an educator.

Section Three

MAKING THE CHANGE

It's worth taking a moment to consider how difficult improvement and innovation can be. The fact that the gap between aspiration and reality for so many educators is large suggests that the problem isn't necessarily a lack of knowledge or imagination. Most teachers have remarkably ambitious and inspiring visions for the experiences they want for their students. They truly want rich and meaningful learning environments worthy of their students' time and energy. However, creating learning environments that help students build their capacity to take on almost impossible problems is difficult work.

While every educator is on their own journey toward that end, very few of us can say we've made it. Instead, we find our classrooms stuck on a particular trajectory, sometimes replicating practices and repeating educational offenses we ourselves may even despise. What keeps us from realizing our true potential as educators? What keeps us from inching closer to our aspirational visions?

What makes change so difficult?

Having a vision for your classroom is of little help without a road map as to how to pursue it. This section will explore three concepts that can make change particularly difficult for educators. First, we will see how our values, priorities, and beliefs can get in our way, without us even realizing it. Second, we will explore the consequences of the "either/or" mentality that most of us bring to our work. Third, we will discuss the role that imaginary barriers play in shaping our perceptions of what is possible and permissible, and what is not.

Finally, we'll explore the role professional goal-setting plays in our professional learning and growth.

Chapter 14

Internal Conflicts

Changing our approach and trying new things can put us in particularly vulnerable positions. Most teachers see themselves as competent professionals, hired to do a critically important job. However, when we experiment with a new class project or give our students even a tiny bit more autonomy, problems arise, classroom chaos can take hold, and we can feel out of control.

Experiences such as these can make us feel anything but professional. In fact, they can make us feel incompetent, ill-equipped, and even guilty for not doing the job we're committed to doing. Our natural instinct to avoid these feelings can keep us from trying new things, even if we think they could be good for us, and for our students, in the long run. Herminia Ibarra, a professor at London Business School who studies leadership and career development, argues that leadership transitions and career advancement can require individuals to move far beyond their comfort zones. For most of us, this doesn't come easy. As Ibarra (2015) argues, "When we are unsure of ourselves or our ability to perform well or measure up in a new setting, we often retreat to familiar behaviors and styles."

When we first recognize that we aren't doing what we say we want to do, it can be easy for us to label ourselves as hypocritical. In fact, we even tell our students to try new things, explore, and take risks. We expect our students to put themselves out there and learn from setbacks, but oftentimes we ourselves don't have the stomach for it. However, labeling ourselves as hypocritical oversimplifies the situation and might not ultimately be very helpful.

Another way to think about this phenomenon is that we are complex individuals with multiple commitments, and some of these commitments may be coming into conflict with one another. Just like Rachel felt stuck between her priorities in the case study from chapter 13, at times we may feel pulled in separate directions. This phenomenon can be described by what leadership experts Ronald Heifetz, Alexander Grashow, and Marty Linsky (2009, 191) refer to as "unspeakable loyalties" and what education and psychology experts Robert Kegan and Lisa Lahey (2009, 36) refer to as "hidden competing commitments."

A teacher may be committed to providing opportunities for her students to collaborate, but she may also be committed to maintaining a sense of control over her classroom (similar to Rachel's case). When the time comes to decide whether or not she will let her students work in collaborative teams, these two commitments may appear in conflict and could influence the choice she ultimately makes.

Another teacher may be committed to cultivating an inquisitive environment where students pose thoughtful questions and pursue their own answers. That same teacher may also be committed to staying on pace with his colleagues, who he knows are covering certain topics at a certain pace. When the teacher is faced with the decision of whether to veer from his plans to engage the class in a discussion around a student's unexpected yet interesting question, or march ahead to make sure he stays on pace with his colleagues, both of these commitments will inevitably compete to influence the teacher's choice.

While we may be aware of some of these conflicts, it's also quite possible that we make many of our decisions on instinct or gut reaction, without fully appreciating the complex set of factors that are having an influence over our actions.

Although it is generally less helpful to think of these commitments as either good or bad, it can be helpful to reach a better understanding of the impact these commitments have on how we feel and how we behave. For example, there are several entirely legitimate and common commitments that may get in the way when we consider trying new things.

Many teachers are committed to feeling successful and maintaining a personal sense of competence. Many teachers are committed to having their colleagues see them as legitimate and responsible. Many teachers are committed to being liked and appreciated by their students and their families and caregivers. Many teachers are committed to maintaining control, order, and predictability in their classrooms.

None of these commitments are inherently good or bad. However, they may, at times, come into conflict with other commitments teachers have and new opportunities they may like to pursue. This conflict makes change more complicated than a question of expertise, skill, or even will—it makes change a deeply personal process.

When you find it difficult to make a change or when your progress toward a goal begins to stall, consider the commitments, beliefs, or perspectives that may be in conflict with your goal.

Naming the conflict can help you analyze your situation in an intentional way, rather than feeling stuck, helpless, and frustrated. For example, rather than feeling guilty for not making progress on your goal to create more opportunities for your students to work collaboratively on complex and meaningful tasks, ask yourself: What other commitments or fears may make the change difficult?

While you may have a commitment to collaborative learning, you may also have a fear that students aren't ready to work effectively with each other. Further, if things go awry, it could make you feel incompetent or inadequate as a teacher and also negatively impact your colleagues' opinions of you.

Once you've identified and named this conflict—a commitment to collaboration versus a commitment to maintaining order, control, and a sense of professional competence—your lack of progress makes perfect sense. You have two forces that are pulling you in different directions. Kegan and Lahey (2009, 39) quote someone describing this tension as if you have, "one foot on the gas and one foot on the brake!"

Naming the conflict can help you better understand what's keeping you from changing, which can actually provide a sense of relief. There's a lot of power in knowing what is happening. Naming the conflict can also be the first step in exploring whether or not it's a genuine conflict. While some conflicts may be real and inevitable, others may not be. For example, you might fear judgment from your colleagues if your attempts at a new project go awry, but you may also come to realize that the vast majority of your colleagues are way too concerned with their own teaching to have any time or interest in passing judgment on you!

Naming the conflict may even help you redefine some of the implicit concepts and beliefs that have been driving your behavior. It's quite possible that you are operating under out-of-date or out-of-whack concepts and beliefs. These beliefs might focus on what you care about, what you are trying to accomplish, or even who you are as a person. As Ibarra (2015) explains, "Consciously or not, we allow our stories, and the images of ourselves that they paint, to guide us in new situations. But the stories can become outdated as we grow, so sometimes it's necessary to alter them dramatically or even to throw them out and start from scratch." For example, consider your conception of "competence." Your fear of things not going well or your desire to avoid feeling incompetent may have served you well at one point but may now be getting in your way. Furthermore, it may also be in direct opposition to what you tell your students to lean into every day! Trying new things, taking risks, and learning from setbacks are all critical parts of the learning process.

Perhaps this internal exploration leads you to *redefine* your concept of "professional competence." Rather than someone who makes no mistakes (your old conception), a professionally competent person is someone who takes thoughtful and calculated risks in service of learning and improvement; professionally competent people learn from their experiences and constantly evolve and grow (your new conception). In that sense, someone who *isn't* exploring and trying new things (and yes, at times, failing) is actually the one who is not professionally competent!

With this new, more thoughtful, nuanced, and sophisticated understanding of what it means to be a professional, your previously powerful internal conflict suddenly becomes far less powerful. Now you can do both—you can try new things *AND* experience setbacks and failure *AND* still see yourself as professionally competent. Mind you, this process is made possible by being able to identify, name, analyze, explore, and potentially redefine the conflicts, beliefs, and concepts that are keeping you from making meaningful progress on your change efforts.

You can imagine an entire host of concepts that might be ripe for exploration, analysis, and redefinition. For example, what does a productive classroom look, feel, and sound like? What constitutes academic rigor in your classroom? What do you want to be known for as a teacher? What are the best ways to authentically assess students? What constitutes success in your classroom? What is student engagement?

Consider:

1. Consider the goals with which you are currently having the most difficulty making progress. For each goal, what commitments may be in conflict with each other?
2. What beliefs or concepts may be ripe for you to explore and potentially redefine? How could redefining these concepts help you create new opportunities to experiment, try new things, and grow?

Chapter 15

Either/Or Mentality

Regardless of how thoughtful and reflective we may try to be, it can still be easy for us to see the world in black and white terms. An either/or mentality can raise the stakes when it comes to trying new things, making change seem far riskier than it may actually be.

Understandably, when faced with a decision to go all in or stay out, our instinct may be to avoid change and stay out. Undoubtedly, there are plenty of teachers who are interested in using more complex and open-ended tasks in their classrooms but won't make any changes because they are too afraid to fully let go of their current, more "traditional" approach to teaching. There are teachers who want to explore different ways to assess their students, such as using performance-based and authentic assessments but don't do so because they aren't willing to give up all of their "traditional" assessments.

However, there is *a lot* of space between a fully "traditional" math class with a lecture and individual practice and a fully project-based learning class with complex tasks and collaborative groups. There is *a lot* of space between a class exclusively using performance assessments and a class exclusively using "traditional" assessments. Yet, as teachers, we tend to place ourselves on one extreme of a false dichotomy, which makes a leap to the other side appear unnecessarily daunting, dramatic, and scary.

This either/or mentality can make change seem bigger than it needs to be, freezing educators in place, keeping them from trying new things.

The either/or mentality can extend to the values, beliefs, and commitments discussed earlier as well. We can get stuck seeing ourselves as someone who is committed to student collaboration or someone committed to control and order, and it's difficult for us to imagine those commitments coexisting. As a result, we fail to venture into new territory because we are unwilling to let go of our commitments, without realizing that our commitments may not need to be in complete conflict. There are plenty of masterful teachers who can balance control and collaboration, finding a space in between that leverages the benefits of each position.

Conversations in education, like many fields, are prone to either/or thinking. Individuals are encouraged to "take a side," pledging allegiance to pure forms of one extreme or the other. Direct instruction or collaborative learning. Strict and firm or warm and welcoming. Grades are good or grades are bad. Standardization or customization. Classes focused on "pure" disciplines or classes that are purely "interdisciplinary."

In reality, there are virtues and benefits to each side of most of these debates, as well as limitations and drawbacks. Consequently, the question isn't: Which is right? The question is: What is the right harmony?

The concept of "polarity management," explored by Barry Johnson in his 2014 book *Polarity Management: Identifying and Managing Unsolvable Problems*, can help us think through questions that tend to be polarizing. On issues where we have a strong preference, we tend to overinflate the virtues of our own side, while overinflating the drawbacks of the other side. We also tend to downplay the drawbacks of our perspective, as well as the benefits of the other. The problem that results is that we can get stuck on one side and never realize the power that comes when we draw on the benefits (and minimize the drawbacks) of each side (Johnson 2014).

Polarities management gives us a way to think more creatively to find harmony between the two poles. First, you need to identify the polarity that may be at play and objectively identify the drawbacks and benefits to each side. If you happen to have a strong preference for one side or the other, enlisting someone with a different perspective can be helpful.

Consider two science teachers, Jean and Mahammad, who are about to embark on a new unit. Jean and Mahammad have very different, and strong, perspectives on the "best" way to proceed. Jean believes that the best approach is to have students replicate a classic science experiment that helps illustrate a specific scientific concept. Mahammad believes that the best approach is to have students design and run their own experiment.

Perhaps these two teachers identify the polarity as "classic versus inquiry." The next step is to identify the benefits of each of the approaches. For example, Jean and Mahammad might identify one benefit of the classic approach to be that students come into close contact with rigorous standards as to how expert scientists design experiments. In doing so, students are more likely to replicate the results that will lead them to draw scientifically sound conclusions. Jean and Mahammad might identify the benefit of the inquiry approach to be that students are more closely engaged in the authentic work of scientists; students are the ones defining the question, designing the experiment, gathering data, and drawing conclusions.

An either/or approach would force Jean and Mahammad to take a stand and determine which of these approaches is better. In reality, there are benefits and drawbacks to each. The task of the teacher is to determine how to create an experience that draws on the best aspects of each approach, while minimizing the drawbacks.

Considering the benefits and drawbacks of each approach, Jean and Mahammad consider other possible ways to proceed. Jean and Mahammad ultimately decide to have students begin by designing their own experiment. However, before students actually conduct their experiments, Jean and Mahammad share the experimental design of the classic experiment.

Students explore what is similar and what is different between their design and the classic design and how those differences might influence the question they are testing, the data they collect, and the conclusions they are able to draw. Then, students undergo a revision process with their own designs, making changes that improve their experiments.

This approach—an approach that draws on both of the original approaches—engages students in the authentic work of scientists while also exposing them to the benefits of the classic experiment.

Jean, who originally favored the classic approach, is now able to engage his students in authentic scientific practices, such as designing and running an experiment. Mahammad, who originally favored the inquiry approach, is now able to expose his students to a rigorously designed experiment, which ideally improves the quality of the student-designed experiments.

By resisting the temptation to stay at their own ends of the spectrum, and through the willingness to explore the benefits of different approaches, both Jean and Mahammad stand to learn and grow. As a result, their students stand to benefit.

Teaching is full of these either/or debates. Grades or no grades? Collaborative work or independent work? Student voice or teacher choice? Traditional assessments or alternative assessments? Usually, we pick a side. In fact, usually our environments encourage us to pick (and defend) our side. Rarely do we find the space in between.

It's important to note that the space in between shouldn't be a compromise, which may reflect a sacrifice on both of the sides. Rather, it should be a substantially *better* solution than either side alone, drawing on the best aspects of each side, while minimizing the drawbacks.

If we truly aspire to create powerful learning environments for students, those capable of building our students' capacity to take on almost impossible problems, we will need to find solutions and innovations that transcend the limited possibilities offered by the poles of these dichotomies. To change our practice and grow as educators, we must identify the instances when we find ourselves trapped in an either/or mentality.

To work beyond an either/or mentality and actively explore each side, we as educators must be willing to consider the virtues of other approaches and the shortcomings of our own. We must be open to growing, and we must be willing to engage with professionals who think differently.

Consider:

1. Consider a question that you may be treating as an either/or choice. What side are you on, and why?
2. Consider a colleague who is on the other side as you and interview them. How do they think about the question differently than you?
3. What are the benefits to each side? What are the drawbacks?
4. What could be a new solution or approach that draws on the benefits (and minimizes the drawbacks) of each side?

Chapter 16

Recognizing Barriers and Constraints

Perhaps not surprisingly, we most frequently tend to cite barriers for change as things that are perceived to be outside of our own control. It's easier to look externally when we are trying to make sense of why change is so difficult.

In the context of schools, there are plenty of things we can point to: district or school policies, standardized tests, and overly burdensome school structures to name a few. These constraints can be very real and can have damaging effects on teachers' abilities to support student learning. Consequently, it would not be fair to write these factors off as nonissues. These factors should be under constant scrutiny, with leaders and decision makers always questioning what is best for students and making changes appropriately.

It may also be true that some of these constraints are illusions and not true barriers. If all of these factors were truly constraining, we wouldn't see the immense variation in the quality, creativity, and innovation in learning experiences that exist from classroom to classroom, *even within a single school*, all supposedly under the same limiting constraints. If external systems and structures constrained our roles as educators to such a great extent, the experience from classroom to classroom would be relatively similar, producing relatively similar results, which we know is generally not the case. In fact, quite the opposite tends to be true.

The trick for us educators is to figure out which barriers are real constraints and which we merely treat as real. Education experts Christine Ortiz and Catherine Pozniak distinguish between design constraints and relics. While design constraints articulate the conditions that must be met in order for a solution to be viable, relics exist simply because they always have and not because of a necessary function they serve.

An example of a classic design constraint for most teachers is the amount of time they have in person with their students. Perhaps a teacher has a particular class for forty-five minutes every day. Even if they wanted to, they couldn't easily change that reality.

A relic is something that might look like a design constraint, but it's actually just a tradition, norm, or expectation that has managed to disguise itself as a true constraint. While a relic may be a common or expected practice, there is no real barrier. Whereas the amount of time for a class period may be a design constraint, *how that time is spent* may be a relic. In some schools, if you were to observe five different classrooms, you might make some assumptions about the constraints that the teachers are under.

For example, after observing five classrooms, you might think there are school policies regarding the arrangement of desks (rows), that class must start with a warm-up problem (a review of the concept from the day before), and that the teacher must be the one to answer all of the questions (but only if students ask them after raising their hands). Indeed, these might be real policies in some school, somewhere.

However, it might also be true that these are simply norms, traditions, and expectations that teachers mostly follow. To do something different might feel like an act of overt defiance of a true constraint, but in reality, it may simply be a departure from a relic.

It's worth noting, however, that the consequences for ignoring a relic can be just as real (and sometimes even more severe) as the consequences of defying an actual constraint. In some schools, norms and traditions have a far greater gravitational pull than actual policies and rules, and the social or professional consequences of being countercultural are severe. Regardless, for some teachers, in some situations, it could be helpful and instructive to explore where those boundaries exist and how real they actually are.

We may need to test the constraints and challenge the relics in order to design the learning experiences powerful enough to support our students as they build their capacity to take on almost impossible problems. It may be true that some of the barriers that have kept us from changing our practice for the better are truly out of our control, but it's also likely that some of them are merely relics, waiting for someone to challenge common practice and break new, innovative ground.

Consider:

1. What are the perceived barriers keeping you from fully realizing your potential as an educator? Try to make an exhaustive list.
2. Of these barriers, which do you think are actual design constraints, and which may merely be relics? How can you test your hypothesis?

Chapter 17

Charting Your Path

Preparing students to take on almost impossible problems is an audacious goal, requiring an equally audacious plan. Aspirations and positive intentions are of little help to students if they aren't backed by an educator's ability and willingness to doggedly pursue them.

Progress in a meaningful direction is difficult without first establishing goals. Achieving specific goals requires specific attention and energy toward specific actions. If a goal is ambitious and meaningful, the specific attention and energy required is likely substantively different than what is currently being expended. If you want to run a marathon and you've never ran one before, you're likely going to have to focus attention and energy in very different ways than you're used to.

While the goal might not require you to expend *more* time and energy, it will likely require that you exert it in a *different* way.

Because progress toward your goal will require you to make changes to what you are currently doing, improvement requires an active choice, starting with the choice of the goal. Teachers should always have a few specific goals in mind, toward which they are actively working. For example, a teacher might have a goal to improve her questioning techniques in large group discussions, a goal to build stronger relationships with the students who feel most disconnected in her class, and a goal to get better at creating and enacting open-ended tasks at least once a week.

Making progress on any of these goals will require her to take actions that she is currently not taking. Without these goals in mind, she is unlikely to do anything differently than she is doing now.

These goals may also require changes, both big and small, to how the teacher sees herself as a person and as an educator. As we've explored previously, this can make the change process a deeply personal one. Because these new behaviors may feel foreign and uncomfortable at first, she may feel inauthentic as she attempts to make changes.

Professor Herminia Ibarra argues that an overly rigid conception of authenticity and a static view of who we are as individuals can keep us from learning and growing. As she writes, "Because going against our natural inclinations can make us feel like impostors, we tend to latch on to authenticity as an excuse for sticking with what's comfortable" (Ibarra 2015). Instead, Ibarra (2015) encourages us to see ourselves as "works in progress" and adopt a "playful attitude" to open up ourselves to more possibilities. Taking this stance to your own development not only provides you with more space to learn and grow as an individual, but it also can help you more quickly find ways to better serve your students. As Ibarra (2015) explains, "It's OK to be inconsistent from one day to the next. That's not being a fake; it's how we experiment to figure out what's right for the new challenges and circumstances we face."

Many others have offered recommendations as to how to effectively set and articulate a goal. Many of these approaches are helpful and, generally speaking, a specific goal is better than a generic one. Regardless of how you frame it, a goal must be accompanied by a plan as to how to get there, as well as some way to know that you're making progress.

The process of creating powerful goals is akin to the process of creating powerful learning experiences: start with the end in mind. What do you want to achieve? Why is it important to you, and how will it help you? What new possibilities will open up to you if you achieve this goal? What will you be able to do then, that you can't do now? What difference will it make for your students, your school, and your community? Finding answers to these questions can help you visualize the potential power of achieving your goal.

Visualizing this power will do more than simply build inspiration and motivation. A clear visualization will also force you to get sharp and specific about what you are trying to do and for what purpose.

Next, you have to consider how you will know if you're making progress toward your goal. What data will help you determine whether or not you've reached your goal? What are the leading indicators? What information should you be gathering and closely tracking along the way? What would constitute meaningful progress, and under what circumstances should you be concerned that progress has stalled? How will you know if what you're doing is actually working? Getting answers to these questions can help ensure that your goal is specific enough to track, and that you can visualize what progress looks like.

Finally, you need to determine what actions you will take to make progress on your goal. What, specifically, will you do differently than what you're doing now? What actions do you believe will have the biggest impact on helping you make progress toward your goal?

Answering these questions can help you articulate your own personal theory of change. A theory of change is your *best current hypothesis* on how your actions will lead to achieving your goal. Often written as a conditional statement, a theory of change can be written in the general form "if . . . then. . . ." For example, "If I do A, B, and C, then X and Y will happen, which will lead to Z, which will then lead to me achieving my goal."

A strongly articulated theory of change is a *testable* theory—you can actually implement it and see if it works. Goal-oriented people tend to revisit their theory of change on a regular basis. As you begin working toward your goal, implementing your planned actions, and tracking your initial results, you will inevitably learn more about the demands of your goal and what it will take to achieve it.

As you learn, you can refine and modify your theory of change. Your theory of change should always articulate your *best current hypothesis* as to how you will reach your goal. In other words, the process of pursuing your goals should make you smarter on what it takes to achieve them.

CREATING A THEORY OF CHANGE—A CASE STUDY

To make this process of setting and pursuing goals more tangible, consider Raul, a teacher who wants to get better at leading powerful and deep full-class discussions. While Raul sees value in engaging his class in discussions on literature, he has found his previous attempts to be rather lackluster. He finds it difficult to engage more than a small handful of voices, doesn't know how to avoid getting into one-on-one conversations with students, and hasn't figured out how to get students to build off of (and push) one another's thinking.

Raul starts his goal-setting process by thinking about the end in mind. What would be different if he were successful, and why does he care so much about this goal? Considering these questions, he discovers that one of the things he cares most about as an educator (and a literary scholar) is rich, thoughtful, and reflective analysis of literature.

Raul believes that the skills needed to make sense of a complex novel are the same skills that help people make sense of their own lives and their world. Ultimately, he wants his students to be thoughtful, creative, curious, and critical. As students develop these skills, he knows that they are able to take on more complex work and construct more sophisticated meaning. For Raul, it's not just about the book, but it's about empowering his students to think, create, reflect, and act. Using the language of this book, Raul wants his students to be able to take on almost impossible problems, and he sees literature as a vehicle for developing the necessary knowledge, skills, and mind-sets to do so.

The best way to develop and hone these skills and mind-sets, so he believes, is to engage in thoughtful discussions where the skills are explicitly practiced.

As Raul gets clearer about why this goal is important to him, he also gets clearer about what his actual goal is. He identifies three components: he wants to get better at supporting students to practice literary analysis skills during full group discussion, he wants to engage a higher percentage of his class during full group discussion, and he wants to find ways to remove himself from the center of the discussion, where all comments and ideas flow through him. In other words, he wants to build his students' sense of ownership over the process, as well as their initiative, communication, and leadership skills.

Notice how this articulation of the goal is far sharper than simply, "I want to get better at leading full class discussions." In fact, Raul also finds this articulation of his goal much more motivating, because he can more clearly see the value to his students if he were to make progress toward achieving it.

Next, Raul considers what progress looks like. Raul determines a few specific indicators that will allow him to answer the question: How will I know if I'm making progress? First, he identifies three specific literary analysis skills and decides that he will keep track of how often they are used by students during full group discussion.

Second, Raul decides that the best way to track progress along the aspect of his goal relating to broader participation is to actually track participation. The higher the percentage of students who contribute, the better, he decides.

Finally, he determines that the best way to see if he's actually removing himself from the center of the conversation is to track how frequently students directly address one another during full group discussions versus addressing him.

Now that Raul has a clear vision for what reaching his goal would look like, along with the evidence he needs in order to determine whether or not he is making progress, he is ready to consider the specific actions he must take in order to make progress. As we discussed earlier, there's no reason to believe that any change will happen unless he makes changes to his own actions.

The first action Raul identifies is to increase the frequency of full group discussions in his classroom. He realizes that a full group discussion once every other week is not nearly enough practice for him and his students to build momentum and realize improvement. He decides to build in three full group discussions every week, starting with ten-minute discussions and eventually building up to twenty-minute discussions.

Next, he decides to create a simple literary analysis graphic organizer to use during full group discussions. This organizer will be helpful to both himself and his students. The organizer describes the three focus skills, provides a brief student-friendly description of each, and includes a place for students to plan and write. Raul plans to make new copies of this graphic organizer for every full group discussion and refer to it frequently when students use the skills.

Raul also decides to explore different discussion protocols to address his participation goals. He identifies two protocols that require all students to participate, some in highly structured ways and some in less structured ways. He's curious to know which one will be most effective at helping him make progress toward his goals.

To track his own progress, Raul decides to video record his classroom once a week. In addition, Raul encourages other teachers to observe his full group discussions. When he watches the recordings, he keeps track of the things he identified as leading indicators and asks his colleagues to do the same when they observe. The fact that Raul has gotten so sharp with his goals makes it easy for him to answer the question every teacher asks before they observe: Is there something specific you want me to look for?

Raul can summarize his entire approach in a clear theory of change: "If I identify a small set of literary analysis skills, develop a student-friendly resource aligned with those skills and support students to use the tool, and engage students in more frequent practice by having more frequent full group discussions that are structured using specific protocols, then I expect that students will more frequently practice using the skills, that a higher number of students will participate and engage, and that the discussion will be less centered on me, ultimately building my capacity to lead a powerful full group discussion." Raul writes his personal theory of change on a piece of paper and tapes it to his desk. He appreciates the constant personal reminder about the goal, and also likes the idea that his students know that even he, the teacher, is working on an improvement goal.

As Raul begins his work, he will inevitably learn about the strength of his theory. For instance, his student-friendly literary analysis tool may be helpful to some students, but it might also be confusing for others. Some discussion protocols might work better than others. He might realize that debriefing each full group discussion with his class is a critical element of helping students build their skills, and something he had completely left out of his initial theory of change.

In other words, as he pursues his goal, Raul will get smarter about what it takes to actually make progress toward his goal. As Raul learns and makes progress, he can make revisions to his theory of change to articulate his new, more sophisticated understanding of what it takes to get better. Raul decides to keep the original paper with his initial theory of change and simply add to it. Using different colored pens, he crosses things out, inserts new ideas, and adds footnotes. This allows him to visualize how his understanding about his goal has changed throughout the process. Raul's students and fellow teachers grow more curious and ask more questions about his theory of change and his progress.

Since Raul identified a specific goal and several leading indicators, he is able to track his progress and observe his improvement. Even modest changes that Raul would have missed had he not been looking (e.g., three additional students participating who usually don't) provide him with the encouragement and inspiration to keep working.

Having ambitious goals for our students will require us to have ambitious goals for ourselves. If we hope to make meaningful changes to our students' learning experiences, we will have to commit ourselves to make meaningful changes to our own teaching practice. We are more likely to grow and improve when we are clear on what we are trying to achieve, when we identify specific actions that we believe will help us make progress, and when we monitor our efforts and learn and adjust along the way.

Consider:

Visualizing Your Goal

1. What do you want to achieve?
2. Why is it important, and how will it help you?
3. What new possibilities will achieving this goal open up for you, your classroom, your school, and your students?
4. What will you be able to do then that you can't do now?

Tracking and Monitoring Your Progress

1. What data will help you determine whether or not you've reached your goal?
2. What are the leading indicators?
3. What information should you be gathering and closely tracking along the way?
4. What would constitute meaningful progress, and under what circumstances should you be concerned that progress has stalled?
5. How do you know that what you're doing is actually working?

Developing a Theory of Change and an Action Plan

1. What, specifically, will you do differently than what you're doing now?
2. What actions do you believe will have the biggest impact on helping you make progress toward your goal?
3. What is your theory of change, articulated as an "if . . . then . . ." statement, that describes your best current hypothesis of how to achieve your goal?
4. What is your plan to revisit, refine, and modify your theory of change?

Chapter 18

Finding Ways to Flourish

It's rather astounding to consider the wide range of emotions teachers can experience on a regular basis. Perhaps it's a personal bias, but it seems like the range and intensity of these emotions are unique among professions. In a given class period, a teacher can easily experience elation as they finally see a student experience a breakthrough, and utter frustration and despair as they fail to reach and engage another student. Teaching is a remarkably emotional, personal, and intense experience. For many of us, this is one of the reasons why it can also be incredibly rewarding.

In a recent workshop, preservice teachers were asked to raise their hand if they have had a scary dream or nightmare about teaching. Nearly every person raised their hand. They had only been in the classroom for a few short weeks. Without doubt, teaching is intense.

The intensity of teaching can have a truly positive impact on those who choose the profession and are fortunate enough to become educators. The intensity can make the job exciting, meaningful, and dynamic. The intensity can remind us of the power behind our work.

While it's unlikely, and perhaps not desirable, to make teaching less intense, many teachers might benefit from exploring how to better navigate that intensity.

Severe problems with teacher attrition, burnout, and stress are well documented. Unfortunately, these patterns can be more common in schools serving higher proportions of students of color and students from low-income families, which can have a negative and inequitable impact on those schools and students. According to the technical assistance bulletin "Trauma-Informed Classrooms" by the School-Justice Partnership National Resource Center and the National Council of Juvenile and Family Court Judges, teachers can develop secondary traumatic stress due to their exposure working with youth who have experienced trauma. To address this stress, the bulletin recommends several self-care strategies for educators, such as prioritizing sleep, nutrition, and exercise; taking breaks; connecting with supportive individuals; and engaging in activities that support mindfulness (Pickens and Tschopp 2017).

For teachers to have the most positive impact on students, preparing them to take on almost impossible problems, teachers must also set themselves up for long-term success. The difference between a dissatisfied teacher and a flourishing teacher is great—not only for that teacher but also for his students.

When we reflect on some of the most powerful learning experiences we ourselves have had as students, they likely came from teachers who were engaged and thriving. Unfortunately, the inverse is also likely true. When teachers are struggling, it's less likely that they are able to create the types of experiences our students need and deserve.

Fortunately, there is quite a bit of research on job satisfaction, well-being, and motivation in both education and in other fields. The research has illuminated an interesting dynamic: the factors that lead to dissatisfaction are not the opposite of the factors that lead to satisfaction. In other words, even if you could eliminate all of the things that frustrate and demotivate you in your current workplace, it's not likely that you will be any more satisfied or motivated. Rather, it just means you will be less dissatisfied.

While being less dissatisfied might be an important and necessary start, it's certainly not the end. For teachers to thrive, and for students to benefit, we all need to be working toward increasing our sense of fulfillment and satisfaction with our work.

Herzberg's Motivation-Hygiene Theory distinguishes between two factors: hygiene factors and motivation factors (Adair 2011). Hygiene factors are things such as your work conditions, salary, security, your relationship with your supervisor, and company policies and bureaucracy. When these things are off, you are more likely to feel dissatisfied. While quite a bit of research on job satisfaction is done outside of the field of education, it doesn't take much imagination to see how these factors play out in schools.

The quality of working conditions, compensation, security, collegial and supervisory relationships, and school and district policies can vary dramatically from school to school. As intuition would suggest, and as many teachers know firsthand, when these factors are not in a good place, teachers can feel dismayed, discouraged, and dissatisfied. Sometimes, teachers may even leave their school or the entire profession. These factors can also influence the likelihood that others will want to join.

Many schools and districts put great effort into addressing these factors. Some have experienced progress and success, in spite of how difficult and complicated these factors can be.

However, even when these factors are where they should be, they are not powerful enough to make you feel motivated in your job. The second set of factors are motivators, which includes elements such as responsibility, recognition, achievement, and the nature of the work itself.

Many educators can be quick to point out the things that frustrate them the most about their current working conditions, and they are right to do so. Ineffective or burdensome policies, poor supervision and administrative support, and low salaries, all contribute to dissatisfaction. It's incredibly important for these things to be tended to, to ensure we create the best possible likelihood that teachers are well positioned to provide rich and meaningful learning experiences for their students.

It's dangerous, however, for us to take the "if only . . ." approach toward a quest for satisfaction. "If only these 'hygiene factors' were better" isn't enough to move us toward a more motivated and satisfied self. While many teachers may not have much direct control over the hygiene factors in their school, there is still work they can do.

Martin Seligman, director of the Positive Psychology Center at the University of Pennsylvania, studies the concept of well-being. In his 2011 book *Flourish*, Seligman introduced five elements of well-being: positive emotion, engagement, relationships, meaning, and accomplishment, summarized by the acronym "PERMA."

Teachers can use the PERMA framework to understand the aspects of their professional and personal lives that are likely contributing to their well-being, as well as uncover some areas in which extra attention and improvement could be helpful. This framework may also prove insightful for educational leaders, as they attempt to audit and understand the current state of well-being and satisfaction within their organizations.

POSITIVE EMOTION

While not all emotions are positive in the daily work of an educator, educators can do themselves a favor by reflecting on the positive experiences that do occur. Sharing positive stories about classes, students, and parent and guardian interactions with colleagues may seem countercultural, particularly in schools where there is a norm around sharing professional horror stories. While venting in the faculty cafeteria or teacher lounge may feel cathartic, it also has the impact of reflecting on and rehashing negative emotions, which isn't likely to produce positive well-being outcomes in the long run.

This doesn't necessarily mean ignoring the bad. Quite the opposite, it simply means don't ignore the good. Actively searching for those positive moments and emotions and spending time reflecting on them are daily practices for many who attempt to be disciplined in their pursuit of greater well-being. In fact, research suggests that making a routine of reflecting on things for which you are grateful can increase your well-being (Emmons and McCullough 2003). Some teachers may choose to do this by creating a journal where they document positive interactions, or collecting notes, letters, and emails from students, family members, and colleagues.

ENGAGEMENT

We experience greater levels of engagement when we lean in to challenge, not when we shy away from it. That's because engagement happens when we bring our best strengths to our challenges, according to Seligman.

While teaching provides no shortage of challenges, teachers don't always find ways to meet those challenges with their personal strengths. Whether our greatest strength is our humor, creativity, ability to connect, or ability to inspire, too many of us fail to find a way to bring that aspect of ourselves to our work as educators. Instead, we rely on a cookie cutter image of a teacher, requiring us to fit ourselves into a predetermined mold rather than designing our role in a way that best leverages all that we have to offer.

Teachers who can find more ways to bring themselves and their strengths to the table, particularly to aspects of their teaching that are the most challenging, may find themselves ultimately more engaged with their work.

Clearly, there are plenty of elements of the cookie cutter image of a teacher that all teachers ought to embrace, whether they are currently personal strengths or not. Just because you don't see yourself as an organized person doesn't give you an excuse to not be organized when you're responsible for 150 human beings. However, the cookie cutter image of a teacher may represent the floor, not the ceiling. Educators will feel more engaged when they find ways to bring their best selves to their greatest challenges at work.

RELATIONSHIPS

Many teachers, particularly those who feel compelled by the aspirational vision of education that is outlined in this book, tout the importance of collaboration with their students. The problems that are most important to solve are those on which we must work together, so we say. However, far fewer teachers actually apply the same principle to their own professional practice.

Collaboration among teachers in many schools is lackluster at best and nonexistent or toxic at worst. Typically, the fault does not rest squarely on the teachers. Most of our schools are simply not designed to promote teacher collaboration, where personal and professional relationships can be built among colleagues. A lack of time, an abundance of responsibilities, and conflicting teaching schedules often get in the way. School leaders and teachers must make teacher collaboration a priority. As educational researcher and leader Linda Darling-Hammond (2012) argues, "What great schools, great principals, and great school teams know is that you support teachers by structuring group collaboration for planning curriculum, by building professional learning communities, by encouraging ongoing inquiry into practice."

The lack of teacher collaboration doesn't only have a negative impact on the professional growth of teachers (and the quality of educational experiences created for students); it also affects our well-being. Meaningful relationships allow us to share in the joys, challenges, and successes of our work. Teachers, and school leaders, must find ways to facilitate meaningful interaction and collaboration among educators.

While some schools may be able to facilitate this sort of collaboration and relationship-building in intensive and intentional ways, other teachers may need to rely on their own initiative and creativity to make it happen. Whether it's a five-minute morning check-in, a lunch with colleagues, or brainstorming around some challenges with a colleague over an early morning cup of coffee, finding ways to build meaningful relationships is a critical component of well-being.

MEANING

Seligman describes meaning as a connection to something that you believe to be bigger than yourself. For many educators, finding this connection, at least theoretically, is not difficult. Indeed, most of us entered the field of education because of the profound importance it has for our students, our communities, and our society. The daily opportunity to contribute to other people's lives in significant ways is truly an amazing thing.

On a more micro level, finding meaning can sometimes be a greater challenge. Finding meaning on a day-to-day basis can be difficult when teachers are overwhelmed with the immense practical and logistical aspects of their jobs. It can be difficult to draw a clear connection between greater purpose and some of the mundane aspects of a teacher's daily routine.

Consequently, teachers can easily become disillusioned and lose focus on what brought them to the profession in the first place. Teachers who find ways to keep their purpose at the center of their work on a regular basis are more likely to experience a sense of meaning in their teaching.

While many teachers rely on the successful stories of graduates for inspiration, teachers can find more immediate value through the meaning students experience in their work here and now. When teachers create opportunities for students to grapple with complex and significant challenges and dilemmas, the work of a teacher isn't solely a long-term investment; the returns can be seen immediately. Creating learning experiences that support students to develop the knowledge, skills, and mind-sets required to take on almost impossible problems can provide a tremendous sense of meaning in the moment, for both students and teachers.

ACCOMPLISHMENT

The final contributing factor to a flourishing life is accomplishment, according to Seligman. Individuals must feel a sense of efficacy and experience moments of success. However, the nature of success matters. While at one point in your life you may have felt a great sense of accomplishment for completing a certain task, now you may fail to experience the same fulfillment that you once did. That's because a true sense of accomplishment comes when we are working at the edge of our abilities.

After a few years, or more for some of us, many of the basic aspects of teaching become routine. We've grown proficient at some things and may have backed off of the things we weren't initially good at. While we may feel a sense of competence, we aren't really stretching and growing. We don't necessarily feel accomplished.

Since true accomplishment requires us to work at the edge of our abilities, we need to constantly be stretching and growing. Teachers must ask themselves: What is the next frontier of my teaching? What new challenge can I take on? While these questions are frequently directed toward our students, we need to start directing them toward ourselves, as well. In doing so, we give ourselves more opportunities to learn, struggle, and experience the type of accomplishment that is only reachable when we are breaking new ground.

SEEING THE WHOLE PICTURE

To see how these elements come together, let's consider the two teachers described in the previous chapters of this book. First, consider Rachel, the teacher who is attempting to redesign her unit on the Civil War.

While Rachel might feel competent and safe with her previous, lecture-based, approach to her unit, teaching in that sort of way is certainly not stretching her at this point in her career. Even though she feels confident, she likely doesn't feel a sense of accomplishment. That's because she's not working at the frontier of her abilities—she's not stretching and trying new things. Rachel's decision to create a collaborative and experiential unit with a performance assessment is certainly new. Her decision to mix things up this time around is a good start toward stretching herself.

While Rachel is clearly passionate and knowledgeable about the content and what goes into strong historical analysis, she hasn't previously brought those strengths to bear on this particular unit. By finding ways to support students to build historical thinking and arguing skills, she's calling upon her personal strengths, which will likely lead to her feeling more engaged.

Since Rachel ultimately cares about her students' ability to assess and analyze documents, construct arguments, and engage in thoughtful discussions, this unit will likely give her a far greater sense of meaning than her previous unit did. Rather than simply trying to instill facts and figures into her students' heads, she is now working toward building their capacity to think about and analyze really complicated questions. She's developing her student's capacity to take on almost impossible problems. It's far easier for Rachel to feel energized with this new focus.

While it's likely that Rachel will struggle and stumble as she encounters challenges and roadblocks that she hadn't anticipated, Rachel is also likely to experience some moments of success. She'll do herself a favor by relishing in these positive moments and emotions and reflecting on the positive experiences her students encounter. By reflecting on the things that went well, and learning from the things that need to be improved, Rachel is far more likely to dive in once again in the future.

Sharing her successes, and challenges, with colleagues might also help her strengthen her professional relationships. Perhaps she'll gain a new ally in her department. Inspired by her first attempt at designing and implementing a less-traditional unit, a colleague might be interested in working with her the next time around.

Now let's turn to Raul, who set the ambitious professional goal of getting better at facilitating powerful full group discussions.

Almost immediately, Raul may feel more excited about his teaching because his practice begins to more closely align with his values. Ultimately, Raul believes that students who build their literary analysis skills become more empowered to better understand themselves and their world. The fact that he has an active plan to engage his students more frequently in that kind of work gives his work as an educator a greater sense of meaning.

While Raul loves literature, he struggles with facilitating large group discussions. However, working at the edge of his abilities is precisely what he needs to do in order to learn and grow. After visualizing what it would be like if he were to achieve his goal, Raul can imagine the true sense of accomplishment he'll feel as he makes progress.

As he seeks resources and feedback from his colleagues, Raul may strengthen his professional relationships, leading him to feel more connected to his school and to his work as a professional. Perhaps his colleagues will feel more comfortable reaching out to him for help, and he'll be able to return the favor.

Both of these educators have committed themselves to ambitious goals. If accomplished, there's little doubt that the change in their teaching practice will improve the learning experiences for their students. It would be irresponsible and unhelpful to downplay the complexity and challenge inherent in the work that lay ahead for Rachel and Raul. By committing to these goals, these teachers are also committing to a whole host of challenges that they will need to face.

To make progress, these teachers may need to do personal work, uncovering personal commitments that were previously hidden, which may be working against their goals. By taking on these goals, Rachel and Raul are more or less signing up for an entire set of uncomfortable experiences and emotions: failure, frustration, and feeling incompetent, to name a few.

Rachel and Raul may also face some social and professional consequences for attempting something new. Whether questions come from students, families and caregivers, or colleagues or supervisors, they may face criticism and heavy skepticism about what they are doing and why. They may struggle to find the balance of being open to the criticism while also staying true to their values and principles.

There may be times, during the process, when they question whether or not all of the work—physical, mental, and emotional—is worth it.

However, considering the elements that lead to well-being—positive emotion, engagement, relationships, meaning, and achievement—engaging and pursuing ambitious and meaningful goals may be precisely what they need.

Teachers strive for their classrooms to be rich and meaningful learning environments for their students. For that to be the case, the classroom must also be a rich and meaningful learning environment for the teacher.

Consider:

1. What impact, if any, do your students' life experiences have on your own personal levels of stress and well-being? What supports do you need to pursue to set yourself up for long-term success?
2. If you were to do a personal audit of your professional life, how would you rank the current status of the five elements of PERMA: positive emotion, engagement, relationships, meaning, and accomplishment?

3. In the areas that are currently the strongest, what factors are contributing to their strength? How can you ensure those factors are sustained?
4. In the areas that are currently the weakest, what factors are contributing? What is missing? What changes are you able and willing to make?

Conclusion

A colleague once shared a useful analogy. There is *rowing* work, and there is *steering* work. It's important to know when to do each type of work. If a rower spends all of her effort rowing, she might not end up where she wants to be. Alternatively, if she only focuses on the direction in which the boat is pointed, she'll sit still in the water.

Making meaningful progress on anything requires both rowing and steering.

The first section of this book was about steering. Having a clear vision for teaching is absolutely necessary. When we reflect on our personal experiences, we tend to be most effective when we are clearest about what we are trying to do. That's not to say that your destination should never change. Indeed, a change in desired destination could reflect powerful growth and learning as an educator. Engaging with yourself and your colleagues in an ongoing dialogue around purpose, vision, and goals can help you get sharper on what your role should be as an educator.

When we leave our purpose, vision, and goals implicit or unsaid, we never have the opportunity to critique, defend, or test our underpinning values and assumptions. We must be bold enough to start an initial course and brave enough to change course as we learn and grow.

The second and third sections of this book were about rowing. Inspiring ideas and good intentions are of little help to our students, unless we find ways to realize them. The work of realizing our aspirational visions is difficult. It is the work of rowing. Rapids, competing currents, and sore and tired muscles will be common features of our journeys. However, as educators with profound responsibilities, we must constantly work to narrow the gap between our aspirational visions and our current realities.

In the daily realities of our work, there will be plenty of moments of intense rowing. However, we can never assume that just because our muscles are sore and our arms are tired that we're actually moving in the right direction. Our colleagues, our communities, and, of course, our students can help us chart and adjust our course forward.

For the future president sitting in your classroom, and for everyone else who will live in the world we together will create, let us embrace the uniquely awesome and amazing role we as educators play in shaping our society.

We must be humbled by the responsibility, and grateful for the opportunity.

Compilation of Reflection Questions

Appreciation for Truth and Knowledge

1. How do you help students understand how knowledge is produced within your discipline? How do you engage students in exploring bias and power within your discipline, and whose perspectives and ideas are taken up and whose remain hidden?
2. What opportunities do students have to question claims they see or hear and practice using disciplinary norms to evaluate the truthfulness of those claims?
3. What opportunities do students have to engage firsthand in constructing knowledge, using the approaches, tools, and norms of the disciplines?
4. How do you support students to surface and unpack the underpinning assumptions and beliefs inherent in the claims they, and others, make?

Deep and Critical Thinking

1. To what extent do students' learning tasks require deep and critical thinking?
2. How frequently are students' learning tasks routine? Can the tasks be completed by applying a well-known procedure or looking up the answer?
3. How frequently are students' learning tasks open-ended? Rather than a single correct answer, does the task require students to identify and work through assumptions, considerations, and constraints?
4. How frequently are students' learning tasks complex? Does the task require students to grapple with interdependencies, dilemmas, or apparent contradictions?

Justice and Caring for All

1. Given your goals, what are the ideal sets of rights, responsibilities, and working agreements for your classroom and/or school? What role should students play in defining, living, monitoring, reflecting on, and revising them?
2. What messages do classroom and school practices, norms, and expectations communicate as they relate to the value of diversity, inclusion, and the inherent value of people?
3. What intentional strategies and practices do you employ to develop and nurture a community of learners and a culture that is safe for risk-taking?
4. How does the classroom and/or school model a community capable of taking on complex and collaborative work?
5. How can you support students to draw on their classroom, school, and community experiences to explore the impact that structures and rules have on how people experience a community and work together within it?
6. What systems and structures do you employ to help establish a classroom and/or school norm of respect and care for one another?

Humility and Confidence

1. To build humility, what kinds of meaningful learning experiences would require students to rely on each other in order to succeed?
2. To build confidence, what kinds of meaningful learning experiences would require students to practice working at the edge of their current abilities?
3. How do you help students recognize their strengths and their areas for improvement? How can you use self-assessments, goal-setting routines, and teacher- and peer-coaching to support students as they develop a special mix of humility and confidence?
4. What factors may influence how some students develop humility and confidence? What stereotypes may be at play, and what can you do to actively intervene?

Leadership

1. To what extent do students have genuine opportunities to practice and develop their leadership?
2. What role do students play in identifying and defining problems facing their classroom, school, or community?
3. How do you help students embrace their responsibility and develop their skills at addressing these problems?

Collaboration

1. To what extent do students' learning experiences require them to practice collaboration? Do students solely work together on tasks that don't require collaboration, or do they have opportunities to engage in group-worthy tasks?
2. How do you explicitly teach students to work more effectively with one another? When you observe students working together, what are you looking for, and what kinds of supports (and interventions) do you provide?
3. How do you support students' social-emotional learning, including self-awareness, self-management, social awareness, relationship skills, and responsible decision-making?

Flexibility and Adaptability

1. Are students' learning experiences likely to produce opportunities for them to practice their flexibility and adaptability?
2. When students face a setback, how do you, as an educator, respond? Instead of solving the problem for them, how might you coach them to think through the problem and develop a solution for themselves?
3. How do you support individuals and groups as they encounter challenges, so the messiness of the challenge is used as an opportunity to learn, not a distraction from their learning?
4. What impact might classroom and school policies and practices (e.g., assessment and grading policies and practices, individual and group reflection practices) have on students' opportunities and willingness to practice flexibility and adaptability?

Initiative and Creative Problem-Solving

1. What opportunities do students have to scan their environment, identify problems, and work to build creative solutions?
2. How do you help students develop the discipline to stay longer in the problem-defining space before jumping to solutions?
3. How do you encourage students to take initiative to pursue solutions to problems for which they have passion?

Communication

1. To what extent do students' learning experiences provide them with frequent opportunities to practice their communication?
2. What systems and routines can you develop to provide students with feedback so that they can improve their communication skills?

3. What constitutes effective communication in your discipline or subject area? How is it similar and different from other disciplines or subject areas? What supports can you provide to help students learn to communicate like a mathematician, or a scientist, or a historian, or a journalist, or an artist, or an engineer?
4. To what extent do students' learning experiences provide them with opportunities to practice communication across multiple channels, for multiple purposes, and for multiple audiences?

Curiosity and Asking Good Questions

1. What opportunities do students have to generate and explore their own questions? What support can you provide to help them with question generation and exploration?
2. What problems, questions, conflicts, or dilemmas can you create that are likely to generate student curiosity? How will this curiosity lead to rich and deep learning experiences?

Resilience

1. What patterns do you see between student resilience and the type of work with which students engage? Are students engaging in learning experiences that are worth their resilience?
2. What do you know about your students' passions? What opportunities do you have to coach, encourage, and support them as they pursue them?
3. What are you doing to form strong and supportive relationships with students, particularly those who may have had, or are having, adverse experiences?

Designing a Learning Environment

1. What are the aspirational goals you have for your classroom? In what ways is the form of your classroom aligned, or misaligned, with those goals?
2. What are some of the critical design elements of your classroom? Which elements might be ready for your reexamination, based on the goals you are trying to achieve?

Designing a Learning Environment—Priorities

1. What are your top priorities for yourself, your classroom, and/or your school? To get the full complicated picture, don't be afraid to list priorities that may come in conflict with each other.
2. What opportunities do these priorities help you see, and what opportunities are you likely to miss?

Designing a Learning Environment—Resources

1. What are your classroom's, school's, and/or community's greatest resources? Which of these resources are being leveraged, and which are not?
2. How are your priorities influencing what resources you are able to see? If you were to broaden, narrow, or shift your priorities, what new resources might you see?

Designing a Learning Environment—Processes

1. What are the processes that your classroom and/or school relies on the most? Are these processes effective at leveraging your classroom's resources?
2. What new processes may need to be designed and implemented to fully take advantage of other, previously underutilized, resources?

Making the Change—Internal Conflicts

1. Consider the goals with which you are currently having the most difficulty making progress. For each goal, what commitments may be in conflict with each other?
2. What beliefs or concepts may be ripe for you to explore and potentially redefine? How could redefining these concepts help you create new opportunities to experiment, try new things, and grow?

Making the Change—Either/Or Mentality

1. Consider a question that you may be treating as an either/or choice. What side are you on, and why?
2. Consider a colleague who is on the other side as you, and interview them. How do they think about the question differently than you?
3. What are the benefits to each side? What are the drawbacks?
4. What could be a new solution or approach that draws on the benefits (and minimizes the drawbacks) of each side?

Making the Change—Recognizing Barriers and Constraints

1. What are the perceived barriers keeping you from fully realizing your potential as an educator? Try to make an exhaustive list.
2. Of these barriers, which do you think are actual design constraints, and which may merely be relics? How can you test your hypothesis?

Charting Your Path

Visualizing Your Goal

1. What do you want to achieve?
2. Why is it important, and how will it help you?
3. What new possibilities will achieving this goal open up for you, your classroom, your school, and your students?
4. What will you be able to do then that you can't do now?

Tracking and Monitoring Your Progress

1. What data will help you determine whether or not you've reached your goal?
2. What are the leading indicators?
3. What information should you be gathering and closely tracking along the way?
4. What would constitute meaningful progress, and under what circumstances should you be concerned that progress has stalled?
5. How do you know that what you're doing is actually working?

Developing a Theory of Change and an Action Plan

1. What, specifically, will you do differently than what you're doing now?
2. What actions do you believe will have the biggest impact on helping you make progress toward your goal?
3. What is your theory of change, articulated as an "if . . . then . . ." statement, that describes your best current hypothesis of how to achieve your goal?
4. What is your plan to revisit, refine, and modify your theory of action?

Finding Ways to Flourish

1. What impact, if any, do your students' life experiences have on your own personal levels of stress and well-being? What supports do you need to pursue to set yourself up for long-term success?
2. If you were to do a personal audit of your professional life, how would you rank the current status of the five elements of PERMA: positive emotion, engagement, relationships, meaning, and accomplishment?
3. In the areas that are currently the strongest, what factors are contributing to their strength? How can you ensure those factors are sustained?
4. In the areas that are currently the weakest, what factors are contributing? What is missing? What changes are you able and willing to make?

References

Achebe, Chinua. 1994. "Chinua Achebe, The Art of Fiction No. 139." Interview by Jerome Brooks. *The Paris Review* (133) (Winter). https://www.theparisreview.org/interviews/1720/chinua-achebe-the-art-of-fiction-no-139-chinua-achebe.

Adair, John E. 2011. *The John Adair Lexicon of Leadership: The Definitive Guide to Leadership Skills and Knowledge*. Philadelphia, Pennsylvania and London, United Kingdom: Kogan Page Publishers.

Adichie, Chimamanda Ngozi. 2009. "The Danger of a Single Story." Filmed July 2009 at TEDGlobal 2009. Video, 13:45. https://www.ted.com/talks/chimamanda_adichie_the_danger_of_a_single_story.

American Psychological Association. 2009. "Stereotype Threat Widens Achievement Gap." Accessed March 10, 2019. https://www.apa.org/research/action/stereotype.

Bernstein, Ethan, Jesse Shore, and David Lazer. 2018. "How Intermittent Breaks in Interaction Improve Collective Intelligence." *Proceedings of the National Academy of Sciences of the United States of America* 115 (35) (August): 8734–39. https://doi.org/10.1073/pnas.1802407115.

Boaler, Jo. 2017. "Math Class Doesn't Work. Here's the Solution." *Time*, October 5. http://time.com/4970465/how-to-improve-math-class/.

CASEL. 2017. "Framework for Systemic Social and Emotional Learning." Accessed March 10, 2019. https://casel.org/what-is-sel/.

Center on the Developing Child. n.d. "Resilience." Accessed May 2, 2019. https://developingchild.harvard.edu/science/key-concepts/resilience/.

Cohen, Elizabeth. 1994. *Designing Groupwork: Strategies for the Heterogeneous Classroom*. 2nd Edition. New York: Teachers College Press.

Couger, J. Daniel. 1995. *Creative Problem Solving and Opportunity Finding*. Danvers, MA: Boyd & Fraser Publishing Company, a division of International Thomson Publishing, Inc.

Christensen, Clayton M., and Stephen P. Kaufman. 2006. "Assessing Your Organization's Capabilities: Resources, Processes and Priorities." *Harvard Business School Publishing* Module Note 607–014, September 2006.

Darling-Hammond, Linda. 2012. "The Challenges of Supporting New Teachers: A Conversation with Linda-Darling Hammond." Interview by Marge Scherer. *Educational Leadership* 69 (8) (May): 18–23.

Democratic National Convention. "Barack Obama — DNC 2016 Film." Posted [July 2016]. YouTube video. https://www.youtube.com/watch?v=IhpQzeDX7To

Dewey, John. 1916. *Democracy and Education: An Introduction to the Philosophy of Education*. New York: The Macmillan Company.

Duckworth, Angela. 2017. "Angela Duckworth: 'A Passion Is Developed More than It Is Discovered.'" Interview by Dan Schawbel. *Forbes*. January 9.

Edmondson, Amy C. 2002. "Managing the Risk of Learning: Psychological Safety in Work Teams." March 15. https://www.hbs.edu/faculty/Publication%20Files/02-062_0b5726a8-443d-4629-9e75-736679b870fc.pdf.

Emmons, Robert A, and Michael E McCullough. 2003. "Counting Blessings versus Burdens: An Experimental Investigation of Gratitude and Subjective Well-Being in Daily Life." *Journal of Personality and Social Psychology* 84(2): 377–89, doi:10.1037//0022–3514.84.2.377.

Eye in the Sky. Film. Directed by Gavin Hood. Bleecker Street, 2015.

Fisher, Roger, William Ury, and Bruce Patton. 1991. *Getting to Yes: Negotiating Agreement without Giving In*. 2nd Edition. New York: Penguin Books.

Grant, Adam. 2018. "The Problem with All-Stars*." A TED Original Podcast*, March. https://www.ted.com/talks/worklife_with_adam_grant_the_team_of_humble_stars

Gray, Barbara. 1989. *Collaborating: Finding Common Ground for Multiparty Problems*. California: Jossey-Bass Inc., Publishers.

Heifetz, Ronald, and Marty Linsky. 2002. *Leadership on the Line*. Massachusetts: Harvard Business School Publishing.

Heifetz, Ronald, Alexander Grashow, and Marty Linsky. 2009. *The Practice of Adaptive Leadership*. Boston, MA: Harvard Business Press.

Ibarra, Herminia. 2015. "The Authenticity Paradox." *Harvard Business Review* (January–February): 52–59.

Johnson, Barry. 2014. *Polarity Management: Identifying and Managing Unsolvable Problems*. Amherst, MA: HRD Press, Inc.

Kegan, Robert, and Lisa Laskow Lahey. 2009. *Immunity to Change: How to Overcome It and Unlock the Potential in Yourself and Your Organization*. Boston, MA: Harvard Business Press.

Kohn, Alfie. 1999. *The Schools Our Children Deserve: Moving Beyond Traditional Classrooms and "Tougher Standards."* New York: Houghton Mifflin Company.

Ladson-Billings, Gloria. 2009. *The Dream-Keepers: Successful Teachers of African American Children*. San Francisco, CA: Jossey-Bass.

Lotan, Rachel A. 2003. "Group-Worthy Tasks." *Educational Leadership* 60(6) (March): 72–75.

Lotan, Rachel A. 2004. "Stepping into Groupwork." In *Teaching Cooperative Learning: The Challenge for Teacher Education*, edited by Elizabeth G. Cohen, Celeste M. Brody, and Mara Sapon-Shevin, 167–82. Albany: State University of New York Press.

Noguera, Pedro A. 2008. *The Trouble with Black Boys: . . . and Other Reflections on Race, Equity, and the Future of Public Education.* San Francisco, CA: Jossey-Bass.

Noguera, Pedro A. 2018. "Turn & Talk/Q&A with Pedro Noguera." Interview in *Educational Leadership*, October.

Oakland Unified School District. 2013. "Instructional Toolkit for Mathematics." *Oakland Unified School District: Leadership, Curriculum and Instruction*, 2013–2014.

Owens, Bradley P., Angela S. Wallace, and David A. Waldman. 2015. "Leader Narcissism and Follower Outcomes: The Counterbalancing Effect of Leader Humility." *Journal of Applied Psychology* 100(4), 1203–13. http://dx.doi.org/10.1037/a0038698.

Pickens, Isaiah B., and Nicole Tschopp. 2017. *Trauma-Informed Classrooms.* National Council of Juvenile and Family Court Judges. https://www.ncjfcj.org/sites/default/files/NCJFCJ_SJP_Trauma_Informed_Classrooms_Final.pdf

Program on Negotiation. 2019. "Expanding the Pie: Integrative versus Distributive Bargaining Negotiation Strategies." Accessed March 10, 2019. https://www.pon.harvard.edu/daily/negotiation-skills-daily/negotiation-skills-expanding-the-pie-integrative-bargaining-versus-distributive-bargaining/.

Seligman, Martin E. P. 2011. *Flourish: A Visionary New Understanding of Happiness and Well-Being.* New York: Free Press.

Steele, Claude M. 2010. *Whistling Vivaldi: How Stereotypes Affect Us and What We Can Do.* New York: W. W. Norton & Company, Inc.

Thigpen, Tyler. 2018. "Everything Changes When You Ask Students: How Did Your Work Help Someone Else?" *Atlanta Journal-Constitution*, January 28. https://www.ajc.com/blog/get-schooled/everything-changes-when-you-ask-students-how-did-your-work-help-someone-else/6pU2A6nJVNI6sTRv5KZntJ/.

Wagner, Tony. 2012. "Graduating All Students Innovation-Ready." *Education Week*, August 14. https://www.edweek.org/ew/articles/2012/08/14/01wagner.h32.html.

Wedell-Wedellsborg, Thomas. 2017. "Are You Solving the Right Problems?" *Harvard Business Review* (January–February): 76–83.

About the Author

Zachary Herrmann is executive director of the Center for Professional Learning at the University of Pennsylvania Graduate School of Education. Zachary is also a member of the Associated Faculty, and teaches courses on teaching, learning, and leadership. Zachary earned his BS in mathematics from the University of Illinois, and his MA in education from Stanford University. Zachary taught high school mathematics and coached cross country and track. While teaching, Zachary helped form a collaborative network of schools and teachers dedicated to improving teaching practice focused on equitable collaborative learning. Zachary earned his master's in educational administration and leadership from the University of Illinois and his doctorate in education leadership from Harvard University.